BIG LEAGUE BASEBALL

A HISTORY

BIG LEAGUE BASEBALL

A HISTORY

Volume 1: 1871-1893

PAUL DeFonzo

BIG LEAGUE BASEBALL: A HISTORY © 2023 by Paul DeFonzo. All rights reserved. No part of this book may be reproduced, distributed, or transmitted in any form or by any means electronic or mechanical, without the prior written permission of the publisher, except in the case of brief quotations embodied in critical articles and reviews and certain other noncommercial uses permitted by copyright law.

Cover design & illustrations © 2023 by Jesse Loving of Ars Longa Art Cards from 19th century photographic cards, cabinets, and *cartes de visite*, and prints. A full list of the illustrations and their sources are listed in the Appendix to this volume.

ISBN: 978-1-944234-55-3
FIRST EDITION 2024
10 9 8 7 6 5 4 3 2 1

Printed in the United States of America by Last Word Press in Olympia, Washington.

A note on the font:

The font used in this text is Century Gothic. Debuting in 1991, the font's developer is not credited, but its origins are in the Monotype 20th Century design created by the great American typographer Sol Hess between 1936 and 1947. Century Gothic is a sans serif font characterized by neatness, elegance, and readability. For a subject as potentially dense and detailed as the history of baseball, the above referenced characteristics are deemed by the author to be indispensable.

Dedicated to My Friend
Phil Morace
Baseball's Brother-In-Law

CONTENTS

Preface ix

Introduction by Jesse Loving xi

Bibliography to Introduction xxiv

1871 1

1872 6

1873 10

1874 14

1875 18

1876 22

1877 26

1878 30

1879 34

1880 39

1881 44

1882 48

1883 55

1884 61

1885 68

1886 76

1887 83

1888 89

1889 95

1890	103
1891	112
1892	118
1893	123
Epilogue to Volume 1	129
Appendix A – Tabulating Offense	132
Appendix B – Best Hitter by Season	135
Appendix C – Rating Pitchers – Starters	137
Appendix D – Best Starting Pitcher by Season	140
Appendix E – Rating Pitchers – Relievers	142
Appendix F – Assessing Defense	144
Appendix G – Source Materials	147
Appendix H – The Pictures	150
Appendix I – Artwork Credits	152
Bibliography	156

PREFACE

Big league baseball's history is filled with drama. It's 1988 and Dodger Kirk Gibson limps up to the plate in the 9th inning to pinch-hit against future Hall of Famer Dennis Eckersley of Oakland, the stingiest relief pitcher of his time.

Boom.

Most baseball fans from that era have the moment etched into their memory, as well they should. A thrilling, game ending, series altering play on baseball's biggest stage, the World Series, has just occurred.

I wonder, though, how many of those same fans are familiar with an even more dramatic moment from baseball's dusty post-season archive.

It's 1886 and future Hall of Famer John Clarkson of Chicago looks in from the pitcher's box to battery mate Mike 'King' Kelly, another star destined for Cooperstown. This is also a World's Series (note the apostrophe) but before streaming, TV, or even radio. The Series is on the line in extra innings with speedy St. Louis centerfielder Curt Welch bouncing off third, preparing to try to steal home in a tied game. Catcher Kelly anticipates the attempt and prepares to thwart the heist. Here comes the pitch, here comes Welch, the pitch is high…SAFE! St. Louis wins the first undisputed post-season championship in its history, and in the history of the American Association against the older, rival National League.

While Welch's "$15,000 slide" (the approximate winner-take-all total of the purse) ranks as one of the most dramatic moments in baseball history, precious few watching Kirk Gibson pump his fist around the bases 100 years later know anything about it.

The goal of this book is to bring such moments as "the $15,000 slide", bygone stars like Clarkson, Kelly, and Welch, the forgotten 19th century leagues, embarrassing missteps in baseball history such as syndicate baseball and the 1892 split season, as well as the best players from baseball's glorious and generally discarded history back into the popular consciousness.

Together we will trace the history of big league baseball year by year from its inaugural season of 1871 up to the establishment of the modern pitching distance of sixty feet six inches in 1893. We will relive the highlights, lowlights, and growing pains of the game as it evolved from its rudimentary beginnings in the 19th century to the four tiered playoff format of the 21st century, to be addressed in future volumes.

Along the way we will become re-acquainted with the best players by position for each season, long forgotten pennant races and post-season championships, significant rules changes, some statistical analysis, and, most importantly, names which were popular in their time, now to resound again.

Enjoy the spectacle.

Big League Baseball: An Introduction

As its title implies, this book is the first volume of a compendium that chronicles the entire history of big league baseball, season by season. Naturally, the first chapter begins in 1871, the first year of the first fully professional baseball league, the National Association of Professional Base Ball Players (NAPBBP).

In its inaugural season, the NAPBBP hosted nine clubs from nine cities representing six states and Washington, D.C. The clubs employed 115 players and played 127 games before hundreds of thousands of paying spectators, ultimately achieving the goal of crowning the first national champion in American professional team sports history. Yet remarkably, just thirty years prior, there exists almost no written record of baseball; not because too few played it, but because so few thought it noteworthy. How did this happen?

Emerging from a primordial spaghetti of old-world bat, ball, and base games with a dizzying array of permutations, baseball metamorphosed within a single generation from an unremarkable children's folk game into America's National Game and its first homegrown professional sports entertainment industry. From historical obscurity a few decades earlier to its premier all-professional campaign in 1871, baseball's rapid evolution, meteoric growth, and cultural transformation during its Amateur Era is an astonishing and uniquely American story inseparable from that of the extraordinary crucible that forged it.

Baseball was accessible in young America. With homemade or found objects used as bats, balls, and bases, the ubiquity of open land, and simple rules that can accommodate two or more players, the game was favored by children but Americans of any age, gender, or skill could and did play baseball. While play was widespread, efforts to organize baseball didn't occur until the first few decades of the 19th century, in schools and social clubs where boys and men had the time, luxury, and inclination to do so. Bridging child and adulthood, prep schools and colleges provided the ideal environment for the students' gumption and baseball became a communal exercise of shared knowledge and resources in a field lab of fun and fraternity with an unprecedented degree of social and geographical mobility, all of which informed the social clubs that graduates would later found and join.

By the 1820s, social clubs in New York City (today's Lower Manhattan) were playing intramural baseball games in public spaces and would occasionally challenge each other in matches for friendly wagers, such as dinner. While the process of transforming baseball from an unrefined children's pickup game into a sport for adult male recreation was well underway, it wasn't until the late 1830s when these social clubs first transcribed its rules that baseball would take a quantum leap from the nursery to the boardroom. In codifying the game, social clubs spawned baseball clubs that played a more coordinated, transferable, dynamic, and resilient brand of baseball. Better able to absorb innovations that enhanced its quality and discard elements that diminished it, baseball had matured into a sport that steadily increased its entertainment value by continually improving its competitive balance. This was the genesis of the New York Game, modern baseball's direct ancestor.

Arising from its advantageous geography and location, New York City was the epicenter of American progress in the 1800's. A cauldron of national issues, international influences, emerging technologies, and ethnic diversity stirred by dynamic social, political, economic, and cultural forces, New York was the beating heart of an expanding American fabric of interconnected and interdependent forces within which baseball was a fiber.

By 1840, the Industrial Revolution had fueled explosive economic and population growth in New York City, where a burgeoning middle class with an entrepreneurial spirit and an influx of immigration led to rapid urbanization and a rise in nativism that elevated both racial tensions and patriotic zeal. With Americanism a hallmark of the zeitgeist, baseball was endowed with the trait and, like apple pie, would become one of its greatest beneficiaries.

In response to the epidemics and pollution caused by its rapid growth, New York initiated a public health campaign in the 1840s that touted the benefits of outdoor exercise. Little did the doctors, many of whom were members of social clubs, know they had planted such a fertile seed in the young country's subconscious quest for a national pastime. Heeding the call, New Yorkers entertained fads of boxing, ice skating, and gymnastics among others, but each suffered obstacles to widespread adoption. Already a professional sport in America, cricket was the leading candidate. But as an old-country holdover and import known as England's National Pastime, cricket stood little chance of earning that title in America.

As if on cue, advancements in printing technologies in the 1850s created a news industry that birthed daily newspapers, modern journalism, and sportswriters. In this fast–growing medium and highly competitive market, baseball was universally lauded, celebrated, promoted, and propagandized as a healthy, noble, manly, patriotic, and distinctly American endeavor. Sportswriters not only romanticized baseball, helping drive its narrative, shape public opinion, and assimilate it into popular culture, but were amongst its most ardent players and instrumental pioneers who made enduring contributions to the game's rules, vernacular, scoring systems, and statistics. Rarely, if ever, has a grassroots enterprise received or benefitted from so much unsolicited and free media investment and marketing.

Continuous improvements to and expansions of public transportation systems also proved a boon to baseball. When urbanization consumed New York's open spaces in the 1840s, baseball clubs ferried across the Hudson to play at the Elysian Fields in Hoboken, New Jersey. They also ferried across the East River to play clubs in Brooklyn, unwittingly sowing the seeds of a rivalry that would profoundly impact baseball for more than a century thereafter. With the newly built Erie Canal connecting the city to the Great Lakes and a rail system rapidly expanding all-points west, New Yorkers traveled to more places across greater distances in less time and brought the New York Game with them. As public transit systems connected communities geographically and economically, baseball connected them socially and culturally, helping shape and define the era's progressive American spirit.

From the mid-1850s to the outbreak of the Civil War in 1861, baseball's culture changed as rapidly as the game evolved and as dramatically as its popularity spread nationally. By 1856, baseball was widely hailed as America's National Pastime and National Game. And while baseball's transformation from a tenebrous children's game into an organized adult sport was nearly complete, its evolution from a recreational exercise into an entertainment industry was just beginning.

As an intramural sport, baseball was played for recreation, exercise, health, fraternity, fun, and fresh air. As baseball clubs challenged each other in matches, a competitive spirit infiltrated the game; but win, lose, or draw, clubs traditionally hosted elaborate post-game feasts where they and their opponents would celebrate and revel in each other's common bonds rather than their contest's outcome. In fact, clubs were originally more competitive over the pomp of their banquets than the circumstances of their baseball teams. However, as matches multiplied, skill increased, talent concentrated, rivalries intensified, audiences grew, gambling escalated, dailies devoted more ink, and the volume of banquets became cost prohibitive, the values of winning were fast displacing the principles of sportsmanship.

Anecdotal evidence suggests that early forms of professionalism began colonizing the baseball landscape in the mid-1850s. As rumors, murky financial transactions, and suspicious player movements between clubs fueled speculation, skilled mercenaries known as ringers were being induced by clubs to join their baseball teams for important matches. Whereas social clubs had always been reflections of their communities, collectives founded upon common residency, occupation, or affiliation, the recruitment of members for their baseball skill rather than their connection to the coterie was an early death knell for the Amateur Era.

By the late 1850s, social clubs might have multiple ball teams organized so any member could play but would concentrate resources on a "first nine." These teams fast became competitive extensions of the clubs and communities they represented, attracting ever more public interest, private investment, and gambler involvement, which only further fanned flames for competitive advantage through economic stimulus. With pressures mounting, delegates from sixteen New York area clubs met at baseball's first convention in 1857, passing resolutions to both preserve amateurism and abolish match-fixing.

Despite the effort, 1858 would prove to be a watershed year in baseball's march toward professionalism. In the spring, clubs met for a second convention and formed the National Association of Base Ball Players (NABBP). As baseball's first administrative and governing body, the NABBP would ultimately lay the organizational groundwork professionalism would need to take root. Over its thirteen-year history, the NABBP's centralized governance would steadily reduce club autonomy and erode Amateur Era traditions, like ceremoniously honoring one's opponent, while institutionally supplanting such fraternal festivities with individuated pursuits of competitive advantage, bragging rights, and economic gain.

Equally portentous in 1858 was an historic three-game contest at the Fashion Race Course Grounds in Queens, NY. While "benefit games" were occasionally organized as fundraising events, the Fashion Course games were the first to charge admission to cover costs. The series was so lucrative though, its net proceeds were donated to charity so as to maintain baseball's air of amateurism. However innocent the intent, the precedent was set. And as historian Thomas W. Gilbert has opined, "Baseball as an entertainment business and as a profession became an inevitability when the first fans paid to see a game."

From 1858 to the outbreak of war in 1861, baseball grew exponentially. With NABBP membership multiplying from twenty-five New York area clubs to sixty-one representing seven states and Washington, D.C., the New York Game was spreading quickly and widely afield. While historian Richard Hershberger has identified more than 900 baseball clubs founded across America by 1860, a contemporary source estimated there were 10,000 members of baseball clubs in New York State alone. Advancing the cause, Henry Chadwick published baseball's first annual guide in 1860, featuring the New York Game's rules, instructions on how to form a club, and a fill-in-the-blank club constitution.

As baseball's popularity exploded, it attracted ever more gifted athletes who dedicated more time and energy to honing their skills, and whose patronage proved irresistible to clubs vying for a competitive edge. While this influx of talent forced more social club members to convert from players on their baseball teams to patrons of them, quality of play improved, entertainment value increased, financial investment deepened, public interest soared, and the concept of baseball as a product, profession, business, and industry began to coalesce.

In the late 1850s, for example, the Brooklyn Excelsiors recruited players based on skill, poached rival club members, implemented novel exercise and weight training programs for its athletes, and even innovated an early farm and feeder system. With some quietly making baseball their primary occupation, revolvers were players who jumped from club to club at the behest of the highest bidder. Revolving was so common and consequential at the time, newspapers published player movement trackers.

While the NABBP passed a resolution banning player pay at its third annual convention in 1859, the loophole–laden stricture only emboldened clubs to devise more creative ways to skirt the prohibition. Waiving club dues, gifting rewards and prizes, providing free room and board, paying relocation expenses, and securing employment and sinecures were all thinly veiled financial inducements clubs used to lure talent while maintaining amateur status.

As the lines between amateurism and professionalism continued to blur, reading between the lines of two 1860 articles published on consecutive July days in the Troy Daily Whig illuminates both the controversy and the forces stoking it: "The Excelsior Club of Brooklyn, who have pretty well reduced base ball to a science, and who pay their pitcher $500 a year, are making a crusade through the provinces for the purpose of winning laurels." Beyond the author's wry intimation that the Excelsiors had lessened baseball for the purpose of winning with near-religious zeal, the snide aside with which he informs us that their pitcher is a hired gun implies both that professionalism was an open secret and that its inherent inequity amidst amateurism was contentious. For reasons unknown to us but about which we might speculate upon with some confidence, the Whig then issued a subtle but striking retraction the following day: "Their pitcher does not receive $500 a year, but he is a splendid player."

The pitcher was Jim Creighton, baseball's first superstar and possibly its first pure professional. Creighton's legend and legacy in baseball history is fascinating, not merely for his pioneering professionalism, remarkable ability, or tragic death at age twenty-one (apocryphally attributed to an injury sustained while hitting a home run), but perhaps most significantly for his primary role in transforming the pitcher from a toothless lobber with limited defensive value into baseball's principal defender who alone impacts the game to a degree never before or since equaled elsewhere on the field. Whereas baseball's competitive balance once hung between the batter and fielders, Creighton's delivery of a ball with unprecedented velocity, movement, and command instantly recalibrated that balance to stand between the pitcher and batter, forevermore making the strike zone – not the basepaths, the territory over which all future baseball contests would be fought.

The Whig's first quote is also remarkable for its allusion to the Excelsiors' pioneering 1860 tour, baseball's first extended road trip, during which the club traveled 1,000 miles over ten days, winning all six matches they played across upstate New York. The historical import of the tour on both baseball and its path to professionalism cannot be overstated. Here was a club, brazenly recruiting and paying (at least one of its) players, playing a brand of baseball that championed winning through athletic expertise as spectator entertainment, utilizing an expanding transit system to demonstrate the superiority of the New York Game and their mastery of it, showcasing their star attraction before huge audiences, and generating unprecedented publicity locally, regionally, and back home. The Excelsiors then embarked on a tour to Philadelphia and Baltimore, winning both games and successfully promoting their methodical and professional approach to the New York Game outside New York.

Indeed, the Excelsior's road trips were triumphs that answered many questions about baseball's marketability, but raised one significant one: How could the Excelsiors, or any club wishing to follow suit, financially afford to replicate and repeat such tours? Of course, the solution had been provided by the Fashion Course games two years earlier, and it wouldn't be long before somebody connected the dots.

For the NABBP's championship series of 1860 featuring an all-Brooklyn matchup of the Excelsiors versus the Atlantics, nearly fifty thousand spectators attended the three games, demonstrating both intense interest in the local rivalry and the emergence of a potential new customer – the fan. Inspired by these massive crowds and the financial success of the Fashion Course games, businessman William Cammeyer built the Union Grounds in Brooklyn in 1862: the first entirely enclosed baseball park and the first to charge admission. A success, Brooklyn then built baseball's second such park in 1864. Not long thereafter, when players successfully negotiated for shares of the gate receipts, the floodgates of professionalism were quietly but irreversibly pried open.

Beginning in April 1861 and ending in April 1865, the Civil War had a profound but equivocal impact on baseball. While the war stifled organized baseball's momentum, with thousands of players enlisting and hundreds of clubs folding across the country, baseball was still played everywhere and by many, but perhaps most significantly by soldiers, officers, and prisoners of war on both sides of the battle lines. While the New York Game was already the predominant style of baseball outside of New York, the war likely further staked that claim culturally by consolidating and solidifying the New York Game's eminence nationally. As dislocation forced teams drawn from more diverse populations to play together and against each other more than ever before, agreement on the rules was not only a prerequisite of play, but players then took those rules with them everywhere thereafter.

In need of reconciliation and reunification after the war, Americans turned to their National Game in droves. Membership in the NABBP ballooned to 100 clubs in 1865 and doubled year over year to more than 400 clubs in 1867. But despite organized baseball surpassing its prewar momentum, the NABBP would never fulfill its promise of becoming a true "national" association. For not only would all but a few postbellum southern ball clubs refuse to join an association based in the north, but the amateur league would soon be supplanted by its professional offspring.

From 1865 through 1868, as clubs and players circumvented a poorly defined and ill-enforced boundary between amateurism and professionalism, baseball was besieged by conflicting inner forces. With gambling endangering the game's integrity and public's trust, and decrying that gambling and professionalism were inexorably enmeshed, the NABBP instituted progressively stringent rules outlawing professionalism to zero-sum effect. While gambling was an omnipresent scourge the NABBP had scant power to curb, many argued that professionalism would subvert baseball's core value as fair and uncompromised sport; an assertion often promulgated with the fallacy that any man base enough to play for pay would also be the ilk to accept bribes to fix games. In a sea of red herrings, the controversy was a more nuanced slippery slope and complex conflict than such broadsides suggest, and so roundly exploited that professionalism proliferated and prospered in all but name.

As for the nuanced slippery slope…While we tend to interpolate our study of the era with our notion of professionalism, i.e., players who received pecuniary benefits were pros and those who did not were amateurs, that was not the consensus distinction at the time. For example, if a club waived a player's dues or paid his rent, and especially if that player was beset by financial hardship, the club was perceived as fulfilling its mandate to act in the best interest of its membership. This deed not only supported a brother in need, but also fairly recompensed his service to the club's baseball program when he might otherwise have dedicated that effort to earning more income. During the Amateur Era, club–member remuneration was not perceived as professionalism, but rather the mutually beneficial exercise of a noble social contract between brethren. Because such reciprocity embodied the founding principles of community, service, and fraternity that defined the social–club ethos, it was an easy and widely practiced subterfuge used to disguise professionalism.

As for the complex conflict…Baseball's dilemma with professionalism was not about capitalism's corrupting effect on character but its corrosive effect on sportsmanship. After all, baseball's intelligentsia of the time was dominated by men and, moreover, gentlemen of means for whom entrepreneurialism, brotherhood, and loyalty were bedrocks of their Americanism. Their condemnation of professionalism was instead fueled by the rising ranks and vagaries of ringers and revolvers: players who demonstrated no loyalty but to the club offering the most money, jumping from club to club and conspicuously often before big matches. It was just such shameless self-interest and fickle allegiance that critics proffered as proof of capitalism's deleterious effect on sportsmanship. Integrity, principle, loyalty, dedication, and service to something greater than oneself: these were the essential qualities of a gentleman and the defining characteristics of his notion of sportsmanship. Naturally, its founding fathers wanted the baseball fraternity to emulate the virtuous archetype of the "social club gentleman" that they themselves aspired to. And whereas amateurism safeguarded such ideals, professionalism threatened to obliterate them.

By the end of the 1868 season, however, it was clear that the NABBP could not resolve baseball's identity crisis and instead had to adapt to it. As more athletes dedicated themselves to baseball full time, developing greater expertise while spending ever more time in the field and on the road, player compensation became more obligatory than voluntary, further pushing working-class club members from the game into the stands. With costs rising due to player and umpire pay, equipment and uniform purchases, renting fields and ballparks for practices and games, travel expenses, and administrative overhead, clubs increased the number and frequency of games they played to increase gate receipts which only increased player demand for greater compensation. With rampant roster raiding pressuring clubs to pay players or risk losing them, under-the-table compensation and escalating venality threatened to turn baseball into a dark market of loyalty-for-hire mercenaries wherein private enrichment would be pursued at the cost of sportsmanship and competitive advantage could be bought by those with the deepest coffers.

In response to these turbulent trends, the ubiquitous menace of gambling's influence, and multiple sprawling controversies, the NABBP finally established a professional category to provide formal governance of openly professional baseball clubs beginning in 1869.

And as for that sea of red herrings…Having legalized professionalism ostensibly to restore and preserve amateurism while also legitimizing and legislating professionalism, the NABBP ultimately realized that its ban on professionalism had led to the creation of a rogue and clandestine compensation system that, in lieu of enforceable contracts, left clubs unable to secure, protect, or control their investments, a.k.a. players. With professionalism a foregone conclusion, the NABBP's resolution wittingly ensured a degree of club control over its players that the two parties have been fighting over ever since. Unwittingly, the resolution also paved the way for professional baseball to flourish at the cost of the NABBP's own demise.

While twelve teams declared their professional status for the 1869 season, history rarely remembers any but the rightfully deserving Cincinnati Red Stockings. In going undefeated against both amateur and professional opponents, the Red Stockings recorded professional baseball's only perfect season in professional baseball's first season. Serendipitously completed that spring, America's first transcontinental railroad enabled the Red Stockings to become the first team to play on both coasts in the same season. Traveling 12,000 miles coast to coast and from the Great Lakes to the Gulf of Mexico, winning games, hearts, and minds at every stop, the Red Stockings were an unprecedented national sensation and feel-good phenomenon, unequivocally earning America's trust in professional baseball.

Despite the successes of the NABBP's bicameral experiment with amateurism and professionalism, conflicts quickly emerged between the two factions. Amid rising tensions and after just two seasons straddling the divide, baseball splintered into two new associations, one amateur and one professional, effectively dissolving the NABBP.

Founded in 1871, the National Association of Professional Base Ball Players (NAPBBP) was baseball's first fully professional league. As the foundation stone of big league baseball, the establishment of the NAPBBP completed baseball's remarkable transformation from an undistinguished children's pastime into America's first homegrown professional sports entertainment industry. It also delivers us full circle, to the aforementioned starting point for the extraordinary chronicle of big league baseball history you are about to read.

After processing the flattery of Paul DeFonzo's request to help him tell the story of big league baseball by complementing his words with my artwork, I had the privilege of reading an advanced draft of this work. Although Paul begins the book appropriately enough in big league baseball's first season, I couldn't help but feel that I was starting the journey at the end of one fascinating story and in the middle of another. How, I wondered, was there suddenly an entire league of professional baseball players?

Unassumingly, I suggested that Paul might consider writing a brief introduction to answer that question. To which Paul countered with a surprising offer. And now, somewhat to my chagrin, I accepted his invitation without hesitation to write just such an introduction.

But while my work with 19th-century baseball photos had afforded me some education in Amateur Era baseball, I had little notion of the complexity of the story I enlisted to tell. For whenever I thought I had discerned a starting point for baseball's path to professionalism, the mark felt inextricably linked to that which preceded it until I ran out of antecedents. Having set out in search of a big bang, I instead found a river of unintended consequences. And with my account's failure at brevity now jeopardizing my welcome here, I find solace where leadoff hitters do: in knowing that the heart of the order is right behind me!

Like all great baseball historians, Paul DeFonzo possesses that brand of love for baseball that compels him to celebrate and preserve its history. In this book, Paul has surmounted a seemingly impossible task by presenting the most salient storylines from each season with a taut focus that both enlightens and entertains. A culmination of his lifelong passions for baseball and baseball cards that will enrich yours as it has mine, it is my honor to welcome you to Paul DeFonzo's *Big League Baseball: A History*.

Jesse Loving

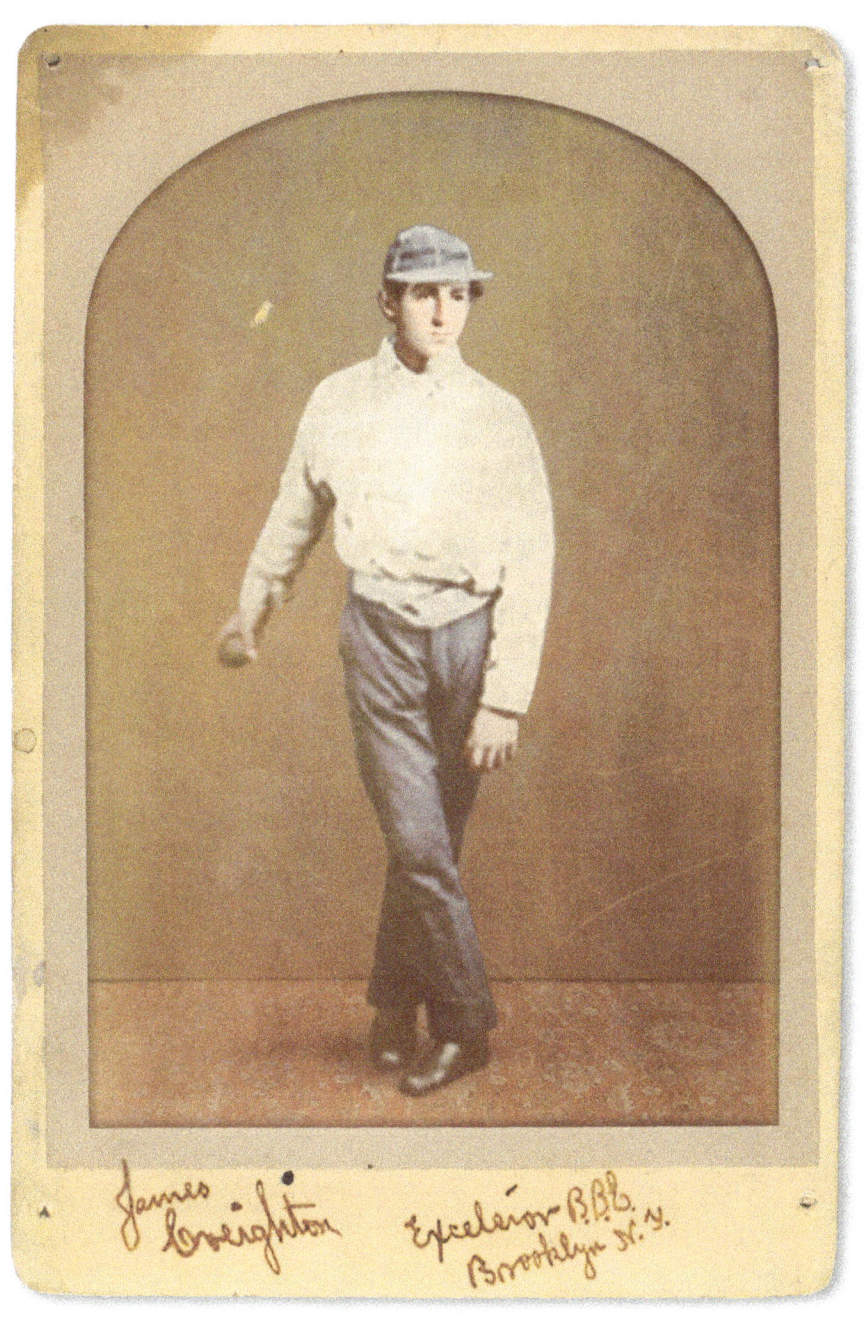

Jim Creighton
Baseball's First Superstar

Bibliography to Introduction

References

vii *Baseball as an entertainment business*: Gilbert, Thomas W., How Baseball Happened: Outrageous Lies Exposed! The True Story Revealed, p.318, Boston: David R. Godine, 2020.

vii *While historian Richard Hershberger*: Hershberger, Richard, "The Antebellum Growth and Spread of the New York Game." Base Ball: A Journal of the Early Game, Vol. 8, Oct. 1, 2014, pp. 134-149, https://web.archive.org/web/20160310070225/https://www.questia.com/library/journal/1P3-3659453141/the-antebellum-growth-and-spread-of-the-new-york-game

vii *A contemporary source*: "The Year 1860." *New York Sunday Mercury*, Dec. 30, 1860, p. 6, https://ourgame.mlblogs.com/the-sunday-mercury-summarizes-the-1860-season-67dc8d4106f

ix *The Excelsior Club of Brooklyn*: "Local Matters: Base Ball." *Troy Daily Whig*, Vol. 26, No. 8013, July 3, 1860, p. 3, col. 5, https://protoball.org/Chronology:Baseball_Professionalism

ix *Their pitcher does not receive*: "Local Matters: Exciting Base Ball Match." *Troy Daily Whig*, Vol. 26, No. 8014, July 4, 1860, p. 3, col. 4, https://protoball.org/Chronology:Baseball_Professionalism

Online Articles

"Ball Play." *New York Clipper*, Vol. vii, No. 32, Nov. 26, 1859, p. 255, https://www.retroseasons.com/library/new-york-clipper/1859-11-26/

Dickson, Marcus W. "1867 Winter Meetings: National Association of Base Ball Players Annual Convention." *Baseball's 19th Century Winter Meetings: 1857-1900*, SABR.org, https://sabr.org/journals/winter-meetings-v3-1857-1900/

Hershberger, Richard. "1857 Winter Meetings: The First Baseball Convention." *Baseball's 19th Century Winter Meetings: 1857-1900*, SABR.org, https://sabr.org/journals/winter-meetings-v3-1857-1900/

Hershberger, Richard. "1871 Winter Meetings: The Winter of Three National Associations." *Baseball's 19th Century Winter Meetings: 1857-1900*, SABR.org, https://sabr.org/journals/winter-meetings-v3-1857-1900/

Koslowski, Jeffrey. "1868 Winter Meetings: 'The Most Brilliant Season' or 'A Lamentable Failure'." *Baseball's 19th Century Winter Meetings: 1857-1900*, SABR.org, https://sabr.org/journals/winter-meetings-v3-1857-1900/

Pestana, Mark. "1869 Winter Meetings: Pivot to Professionalism." *Baseball's 19th Century Winter Meetings: 1857-1900*, SABR.org, https://sabr.org/journals/winter-meetings-v3-1857-1900/

Tholkes, Robert. "1858 Winter Meetings: Building on the Foundation." *Baseball's 19th Century Winter Meetings: 1857-1900*, SABR.org, https://sabr.org/journals/winter-meetings-v3-1857-1900/

Tholkes, Robert. "1859 Winter Meetings: Growing Pains." *Baseball's 19th Century Winter Meetings: 1857-1900*, SABR.org, https://sabr.org/journals/winter-meetings-v3-1857-1900/

Thorn, John. "The Baseball Convention of 1857, a Summary Report." *Our Game*, April 4, 2016, https://ourgame.mlblogs.com/the-baseball-convention-of-1857-a-summary-report-c6b63bee1ed3

Thorn, John. "Last Hurrah for the Cincinnati Red Stockings." *Our Game*, January 8, 2018, https://ourgame.mlblogs.com/last-hurrah-for-the-cincinnati-red-stockings-8f45a7cae59a

Zinn, John G. "1861 Winter Meetings: The National Association of Base Ball Players." *Baseball's 19th Century Winter Meetings: 1857-1900*, SABR.org, https://sabr.org/journals/winter-meetings-v3-1857-1900/

Zinn, John G. "1865 Winter Meetings: National Association of Base Ball Players." *Baseball's 19th Century Winter Meetings: 1857-1900*, SABR.org, https://sabr.org/journals/winter-meetings-v3-1857-1900/

Books

Block, David, Baseball Before We Knew It: A Search for the Roots of the Game, Lincoln, NE: University of Nebraska Press, 2005.

Gilbert, Thomas W., How Baseball Happened: Outrageous Lies Exposed! The True Story Revealed, Boston: David R. Godine, 2020.

Morris, Peter, But Didn't We Have Fun? An Informal History of Baseball's Pioneer Era, 1843-1870, Chicago: Ivan R. Dee, 2008.
Ryczek, William J., Blackguards and Red Stockings: A History of Baseball's National Association, 1871-1875, Jefferson, NC: McFarland & Company, Inc., 2016.

Ryczek, William J., Baseball's First Inning: A History of the National Pastime Through the Civil War, Jefferson, NC: McFarland & Company, Inc., 2009.

Seymour, Harold and Seymour, Dorothy Z., Baseball: The Early Years, New York: Oxford

University Press, 1989.

Thorn, John, <u>Baseball in the Garden of Eden: The Secret History of the Early Game</u>, New York: Simon & Schuster, 2011.

Wright, Marshall D., <u>The National Association of Base Ball Players, 1857-1870</u>, Jefferson, NC: McFarland & Company, Inc., 2000.

<u>Chapters in Edited Books</u>

Bogovich, Richard, The Martyrdom of Jim Creighton. In Felber, Bill, ed., <u>Inventing Baseball: The 100 Greatest Games of the Nineteenth Century</u>, pp. 43-45, Phoenix: Society for American Baseball Research, Inc., 2013.

Morris, Peter, Brooklyn: Introduction. In Morris, Peter and Ryczek, William J. and Finkel, Jan and Levin, Leonard and Malatzky, Richard, eds., <u>Base Ball Founders: The Clubs, Players and Cities of the Northeast That Established the Game</u>, pp. 98-100, Jefferson, NC: McFarland & Company, Inc., 2013.

Ryczek, William J., and Morris, Peter, Excelsior Base Ball Club. In Morris, Peter and Ryczek, William J. and Finkel, Jan and Levin, Leonard and Malatzky, Richard, eds., <u>Base Ball Founders: The Clubs, Players and Cities of the Northeast That Established the Game</u>, pp. 101-111, Jefferson, NC: McFarland & Company, Inc., 2013.

Thorn, John, The Most Important Game in Baseball History? In Felber, Bill, ed., <u>Inventing Baseball: The 100 Greatest Games of the Nineteenth Century</u>, pp. 55-57, Phoenix: Society for American Baseball Research, Inc., 2013.

Waff, Craig B., The Grand Excursion. In Felber, Bill, ed., <u>Inventing Baseball: The 100 Greatest Games of the Nineteenth Century</u>, pp. 24-27, Phoenix: Society for American Baseball Research, Inc., 2013.

Waff, Craig B., and Ryczek, William J., and Morris, Peter, Star Base Ball Club. In Morris, Peter and Ryczek, William J. and Finkel, Jan and Levin, Leonard and Malatzky, Richard, eds., <u>Base Ball Founders: The Clubs, Players and Cities of the Northeast That Established the Game</u>, pp. 144-167, Jefferson, NC: McFarland & Company, Inc., 2013.

Zinn, John, The Rivalry Begins. In Felber, Bill, ed., <u>Inventing Baseball: The 100 Greatest Games of the Nineteenth Century</u>, pp. 10-12, Phoenix: Society for American Baseball Research, Inc., 2013.

<u>Periodicals</u>

Chadwick, Henry. <u>Beadle's Dime Base-Ball Player: A Compendium of the Game</u>, New York: Irwin P. Beadle & Co., 1860.

BIG LEAGUE BASEBALL

A HISTORY

Volume 1: 1871-1893
The Road to Sixty Feet Six Inches

1871

1871 was big league baseball's inaugural season. Prior to 1871 professional baseball teams existed but games were played essentially as challenge matches with no central authority or schedule. The most well known and best of these clubs were the Cincinnati Red Stockings, assembled in 1868 and managed, both on the field and in the front office, by player/manager Harry Wright.

The first league was commonly known as the National Association and lasted from 1871 through 1875. There were franchises in major cities from Boston to Chicago, as well as in smaller cities like Troy, NY, Rockford, IL, and Fort Wayne, IN.

The Association was not well organized and teams folded each season during the five year existence of the league. Furthermore, not that many official games were played and teams did not play a uniform number of games. In 1871 the team playing the most official games played 33. Teams also played exhibitions but these games were not official and did not count in the standings. Exhibitions did, of course, count in the financial ledgers.

There was no post-season championship scheme such as the modern World Series and, in fact, the system of determining the champion was not clear.

The 1871 inaugural season featured nine teams, one of which folded. The first ever game in professional league play was supposed to be a marquee matchup between Boston and Washington, but the game was rained out. These teams were considered early favorites to win the championship since they were composed of many players from Harry Wright's Cincinnati team of professionals from previous years. As a consequence of the rainout the first game ended up matching Cleveland against Fort Wayne in Fort Wayne, Indiana. The Fort Wayne team later folded during the season but did win the first ever game in the first ever organized professional league by what would later be recognized as an unusually low score of 2 – 0.

The race for the pennant in 1871 was a tight one between Philadelphia, Chicago, and Boston. There was, however, a cataclysmic event which impacted the course of the race for the pennant comparable in magnitude to the San Francisco earthquake of 1989, which disrupted the 1989 World Series. On October 8, 1871 the Great Chicago Fire occurred.

1871

Blazing for three days, the fire destroyed most of Chicago, including Lake Park, where the White Stockings were nearly unbeatable, going 13 – 3 to that point. The team elected to play on, but had to play their remaining home games at road locations with borrowed uniforms and equipment.

On October 7, the day before the fire, Philadelphia and Chicago boasted identical 18 – 7 records. Boston's record was complete at 20 – 10 with one tie. After the fire, Philadelphia won its next two, while the beleaguered Chicagoans split two games in Troy.

On October 30 Philadelphia and Chicago met head to head in a critical contest. Although Chicago was designated as the home team, due to the fire the game had to be played in Brooklyn. Before a sparse assemblage of about five hundred fans, the dispirited White Stockings could not muster any offense against Philadelphia ace Dick McBride and lost 4 – 1.

As previously noted, the system for determining the champion in the NA was not clear. Specifically, there existed uncertainty as to whether the team with the most wins, or fewest losses, or most series wins, or fewest series losses would be declared the winner of the pennant. Complicating matters further was the manner in which exhibition games were being counted, how forfeits would be dealt with, and how games involving ineligible players would be handled.

After considerable post-season haggling, Philadelphia was awarded the first professional league championship on the strength of having won the most series. Indeed, the October 30 win over Chicago allowed the Philadelphians to secure both the most series wins, with seven, and the most wins, with twenty one. The Great Chicago Fire likely did decide the winner of the first big league pennant as the White Stockings were knocked off balance by the destruction of their assets, and had to play a decisive "home" game at a road site in Brooklyn, where they generated little fan support.

What follows is a listing of the best offensive and defensive players at their positions as well as the best pitcher in both a starting and relief capacity. Please refer to the appendices on tabulation of statistics for a description of how the scores are determined. Names in boldface denote highest score.

1871

OFFENSE		DEFENSE	
C	Cal McVey – 151 – Boston	C	Fergy Malone – 3 - Philadelphia
1B	Joe Start – 117 – New York	1B	Everett Mills – 4 – Washington
2B	Jimmy Wood – 135 – Chicago	**2B**	**Jimmy Wood – 5 – Chicago**
SS	Davy Force – 121 – Washington	SS	Davy Force – 4 – Washington
3B	Levi Meyerle – 149 – Philadelphia	3B	Harry Schafer/Fred Waterman – 2 – Boston/Washington
LF	Steve King – 138 – Troy	LF	Fred Treacey – 4 – Chicago
RF	Dave Birdsall – 121 – Boston	RF	John Glenn – 4 - Washington
CF	Harry Wright – 116 – Boston	CF	Dave Eggler – 3 – New York
P	Rynie Wolters – 133 – New York	**P**	**Cherokee Fisher – 5 – Rockford**

Multi Ross Barnes – 168 - Boston

Barnes, the most prolific offensive player of the season, ended up without a set position due to injury to the Boston shortstop. Barnes moved from his regular position at second base and took over at shortstop after the injury. Consequently, he did not play enough games at either position individually to qualify as a full-time player at the position but played enough games in the aggregate to have his offensive output considered on a full-time basis.

Best Pitcher: George Zettlein - .926 - Chicago

Best Reliever: Harry Wright - 1.786 – Boston

Since teams were playing a relatively low number of official games and pitchers were throwing underhanded from only forty five feet from the home plate, clubs were able to employ a single starting pitcher for nearly all their contests. Of the two hundred fifty three official games started in 1871, only six were begun with a backup pitcher. On average, each team's number one starting pitcher threw about 90% of his team's innings. Four of the nine teams started only one pitcher all season.

As for relievers, although seven players pitched in relief in 1871, three of them pitched only one inning. Harry Wright, Boston's regular centerfielder and manager, additionally threw eighteen and two thirds innings of relief, second most in the league. Obviously, there was not a lot of relief pitching occurring. That being said, Wright has been credited as deliberately pitching in relief from time to time with the goal of putting batters off balance with his off-speed deliveries after opponents had to contend with Al Spalding's hard stuff all game to that point. This would place Wright as a pioneer in pitching strategy as well as an important catalyst for professionalism and a critical force in the formation of the National Association.

Appropriately, Wright is our first future Hall of Famer to appear on the leaders' board, and at two different positions in the same season.

1871

Dick McBride, who pitched and managed Philadelphia to the first National Association pennant in 1871

One would be hard pressed to find a more pivotal figure in the early years of big league baseball than Harry Wright. Wright organized one of the first pro teams, helped found the National Association, and managed the Boston club to six championships between 1872 and 1878. Seen here as a player, he also starred on the field as a centerfielder and relief or 'change' pitcher.

1872

1872 marked the second year of organized professional league play under the aegis of the National Association. The league continued to be plagued by organizational problems. A number of new teams were added for 1872 but most of them were weak or poorly managed and failed to complete the season. The strong Chicago club of 1871 was prevented from renewing its affiliation with the league due to the extraordinary event of the Great Chicago Fire. Ultimately, only four of the eleven teams which started the 1872 season played enough games to approach the semblance of a full schedule. The highest number of official games played by any team was 58.

Notwithstanding these problems there were two significant developments.

First, the rules regarding pitching were being liberalized to allow the introduction of the curveball into league play. Up until that time pitchers were not permitted to bend the elbow during delivery, which was strictly underhand. The pitcher would now be permitted to bend the elbow, and, effectively, break the wrist during delivery. Although the delivery point of the ball still had to be below the belt, pitchers were always seeking an edge, and many took advantage of lax enforcement by umpires by consistently raising the arm angle to effect a sidearm delivery. This had the dual effect of allowing a curve and, slowly but surely, moving away from a strictly underhand delivery.

The reputed originator of the curveball, William 'Candy' Cummings, was promptly signed by New York. He led the league in innings pitched in 1872 with 488 (not a typo), and by a wide margin over the next prolific hurler.

Besides the underhand delivery, pitching at this time bore little resemblance to what exists in the present day. The pitching distance was only forty five feet from the home plate and pitchers were permitted to move around in a six foot by six foot pitching box, including delivery of the ball with a running start if it suited them. The pitching mound of the present era did not yet exist. As for balls and strikes, a missed swing counted as a strike, as in the present day, but a foul did not. Three strikes resulted in a strikeout but only three balls were required to draw a walk. However, it was up to the umpire when to start calling balls or strikes as the batter was permitted to request high or low pitches and was not obliged to offer at a pitch out of his designated zone. Umpires were frequently at risk of being both verbally and physically abused and were generally inclined to warn pitchers about errant deliveries and batters about letting good ones go by before actually calling balls or strikes. The result of this awkward etiquette was far fewer walks and called strikeouts than we are used to in the present day. Finally, batsmen hit by a pitch were not awarded first base.

The other significant development in 1872 was double edged. On the field Harry Wright's Boston club dominated the league and won the championship by a comfortable margin. The emergence of an undisputed league champion was a great improvement following the uncertainty and controversy of the 1871 championship race which was decided behind closed doors after the conclusion of the season. Unfortunately, the absence of a close race for the championship in 1872 sharply curtailed fan interest over the latter part of the season. Attendance suffered as the handful of teams still playing late in the season did so before sparse crowds. Although attendance data is incomplete for 1872, the league averaged roughly 1,550 fans per game, compared to roughly over 2,600 per game the previous season, which actually featured fewer games.

Here are the league leaders for offense, defense, and pitching by position. Keep in mind that the eligible player pool for 1872 was greatly reduced due to the failure of most of the teams to play a complete schedule. Players on teams which failed to complete most of their scheduled games are not included here for league leader consideration. Only Boston, New York, Philadelphia, and Baltimore fielded full-time squads.

	OFFENSE		DEFENSE
C	Cal McVey – 153 – Boston	C	Nat Hicks – 3 – New York
1B	Joe Start – 156 – New York	1B	Charlie Gould – 2 – Boston
2B	**Ross Barnes – 203 – Boston**	2B	Ross Barnes – 4 – Boston
SS	George Wright – 182 – Boston	**SS**	**George Wright – 6 – Boston**
3B	Cap Anson – 183 – Philadelphia	3B	Harry Schafer – 3 – Boston
LF	Ned Cuthbert – 190 – Philadelphia	LF	Tom York – 4 – Baltimore
RF	Fraley Rogers – 111 – Boston	**RF**	**Fraley Rogers – 6* – Boston**
CF	Dave Eggler – 180 – New York	CF	Dave Eggler – 5 – New York

1872

P   Al Spalding – 170 – Boston   P   Al Spalding – 3 - Boston

Multi Lip Pike – 175 – Baltimore

Best Pitcher: Dick McBride – 1.036 – Philadelphia

Best Relief Pitcher: Harry Wright – 2.039 – Boston

There was still not a lot of relief pitching occurring in the early years of the NA. No one threw more innings in relief that season than Harry Wright's twenty five and two thirds.

Boston's infield dominated defensively in 1872. Excepting the catcher, all Boston infielders, including the pitcher, led at their respective positions in total chances per inning. Despite all those chances, Ross Barnes and George Wright, at second base and shortstop, also led the league in fielding percentage, the percentage of successful, errorless chances divided by the total chances. The accomplishment of Barnes and Wright is all the more remarkable when considering that fielders, excepting the catcher, were playing without gloves.

In the final reckoning, 1872 was a disappointing sophomore year for the NA. There was no race to the championship, too few teams with any staying power, and a significant dip in attendance. George Wright, Cap Anson, and Al Spalding are our newest future Hall of Famers on the leaders' board.

*Only player who played full-time at the position.

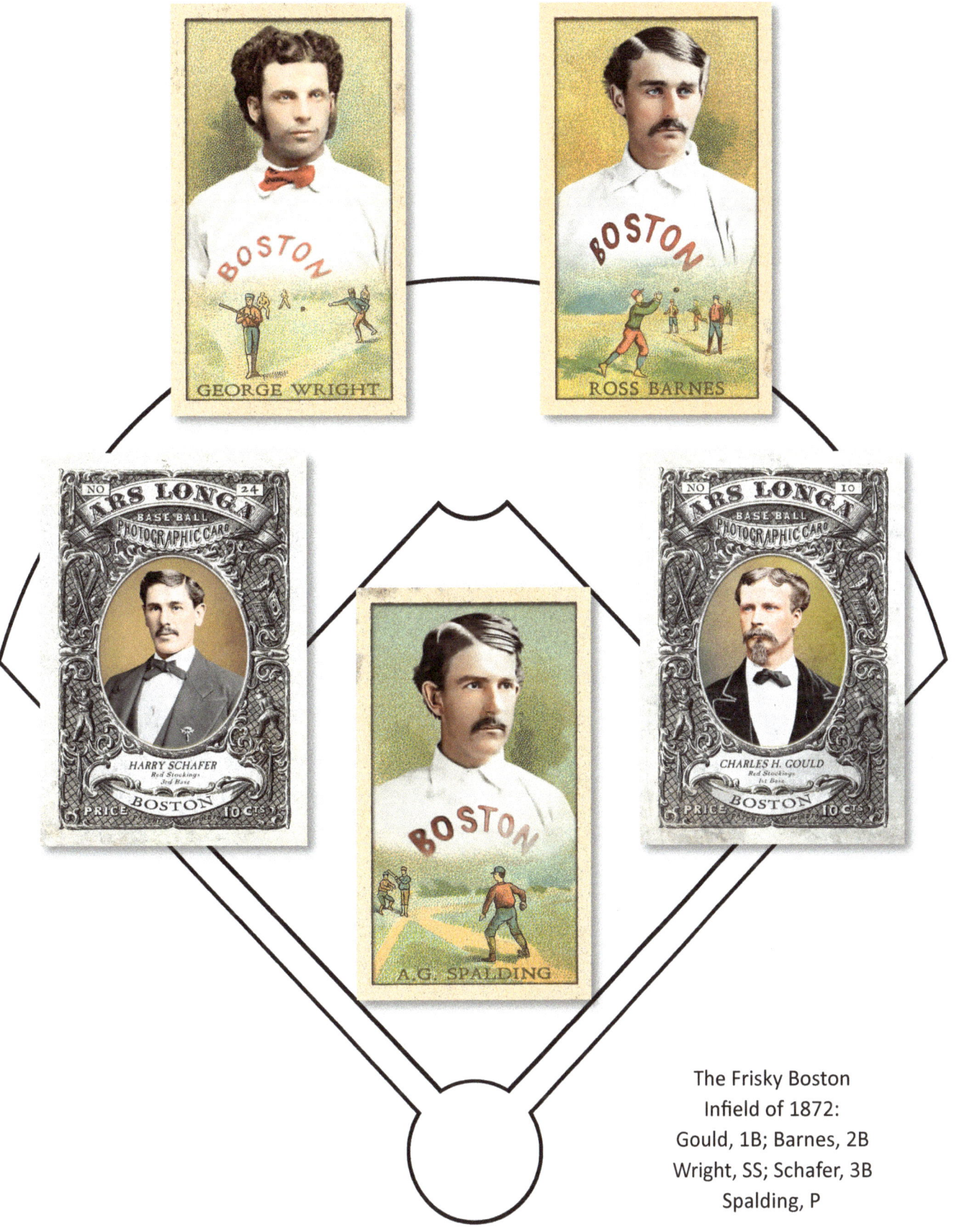

The Frisky Boston
Infield of 1872:
Gould, 1B; Barnes, 2B
Wright, SS; Schafer, 3B
Spalding, P

1873

The National Association entered its third season with two teams competing in Philadelphia, two teams competing in Baltimore, as well as a number of new teams, including one in Elizabeth, New Jersey. Six clubs played complete or near complete schedules. The maximum number of official games played by any team was 60.

The season actually featured a championship race between the new Philadelphia club, the White Stockings, which broke out to an early lead, and Harry Wright's Red Stockings of Boston, the defending champs.

On July 26 Philadelphia achieved its high water mark with a record of 27 – 3, fully ten games ahead of Boston, which languished in fourth place with a record of 17 – 11. Thereafter the fortunes of the two clubs reversed as the Red Stockings commenced a steady climb through the standings. By October 1 Boston had ascended to within one game of the top spot, with 33 victories to Philadelphia's 34. On October 2 the Red Stockings, winners of seven straight, travelled to Philadelphia for a climactic contest with the White Stockings, losers of four in a row.

After three error filled innings Boston led 7 – 5. In the Boston half of the fourth Philadelphia second sacker and field captain Jimmy Wood succumbed to the pressure. Wood melted down on two separate occasions after botched plays while Red Stockings churned around the bases allowing Boston to take an 11 – 5 lead. The six run cushion would prove insurmountable as Boston continued its meteoric rise with an 18 – 7 drubbing of Philadelphia on its home turf.

Although Boston finished the season with 43 wins to Philadelphia's 36, as in 1871, controversy dogged the crowning of the league champion until after the conclusion of the season. The NA rules prohibited the signing of a player for at least sixty days if the player was previously affiliated with another team. Violation of the rule could result in any games in which the offending player participated being forfeited. While the signing of such players was, in fact, commonplace given the high mortality rate of NA teams (three failed to complete their schedules during the season), an aggrieved team was within its rights to lodge a formal complaint.

Such was the case at the conclusion of the 1873 season when Boston was accused of signing outfielder Bob Addy within sixty days of his playing for another club. While there was no question that Boston boasted the best record in the league, wins could be deleted if it was found that Addy was an ineligible player. At this time player contracts were frequently informal and players enjoyed great freedom in walking onto teams or 'revolving' to the detriment of the efficient running of the league. The issue was ultimately decided in favor of Boston but the swirl of controversy regarding the naming of the champion was now becoming a recurring problem.

Here are the best offensive and defensive players for 1873 as well as the best starting pitcher. Pitching splits, which is to say, a pitcher's statistics exclusively as a starter and exclusively as a reliever, are not available for this season, so a determination for best relief pitcher could not be made.

	OFFENSE		DEFENSE
C	Deacon White – 237 – Boston	C	Fergy Malone – 2 – Philadelphia White Stockings
1B	Everett Mills – 184 – Baltimore Canaries	1B	Herman Dehlman/Everett Mills 1 – Brooklyn/Baltimore Canaries
2B	**Ross Barnes – 287 – Boston**	2B	Ross Barnes – 3 – Boston
SS	George Wright – 217 – Boston	SS	George Wright – 4 – Boston
3B	Levi Meyerle – 172 – Philadelphia White Stockings	3B	Bob Ferguson – 2 – Brooklyn
LF	Andy Leonard – 208 – Boston	LF	Count Gedney/Tom York – 3 – New York/Baltimore Canaries
RF	Lip Pike – 183 – Baltimore Canaries	RF	George Bechtel – 3 – Philadelphia White Stockings
CF	Dave Eggler – 179 – New York	CF	Dave Eggler – 2 – New York
P	Al Spalding – 220 – Boston	**P**	**Al Spalding – 5 – Boston**
Multi	Jim O'Rourke – 196 – Boston		

It's not hard to figure out the key to Boston's success in 1873. The Red Stockings boasted the best offensive player at five of nine positions plus O'Rourke shifting between first base and the outfield. Boston outscored the next best offensive team, the Canaries of Baltimore, by better than one run per game.

Ross Barnes was the best offensive player for the third consecutive season, and by a considerable margin.

Best Starting Pitcher – Bobby Mathews - .956 – New York

Best Relief Pitcher – TBD

Spalding of Boston finished second for best pitcher for the third consecutive season. He was, however, the best athlete at the position, with an offensive score over eighty points better than his nearest rival, and by far the best fielder at the position.

1873 was certainly an improvement over the dismal 1872 season for the NA. More teams survived the season and there was an exciting race for the championship. It was clear, however, that the problems of team viability and player movement were persisting in preventing the league from operating smoothly. Furthermore, there was a delay in naming the champion for the second time in the league's first three seasons.

"Orator" Jim O'Rourke and Deacon White appear as our newest future Hall of Famers on the leaders' board.

Bob Addy, whose presence on the Red Stockings nearly cost them the pennant in 1873

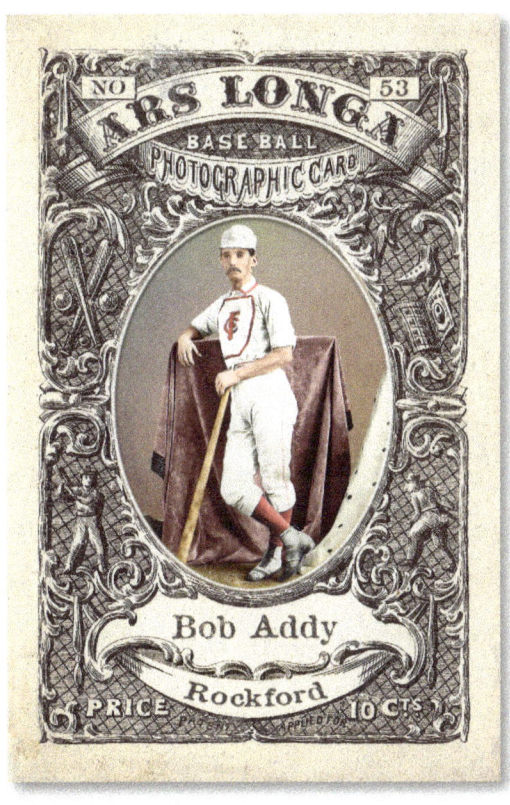

1873

Al Spalding, Boston's star pitcher of the early 1870's, whose story is the story of big league baseball in the 19th century.

Pitching ace, athlete, manager, owner, league spokesman, goodwill ambassador, sporting goods impresario, Spalding played every part in the baseball business and was most responsible for establishing the National League as the dominant league until the 20th century.

1874

1874 featured the return of Chicago to the NA roster of clubs while Washington did not field a team for the first time since the founding of the league. Seven of the eight competing teams completed a full schedule in 1874. The maximum number of games played by any team was 71, the most ever.

1874 also marked the first year that professional baseball took the show across the pond. In July the first place Red Stockings of Boston and the second place Athletics of Philadelphia embarked on a trans-Atlantic voyage to the United Kingdom for a series of exhibitions against each other as well as contests of cricket and baseball with their hosts. Thus began the tradition of major league baseball showcasing itself away from North America, a tradition which continues to the present day.

The absence of the first and second place clubs from the United States in July and August did impact the pennant race. During the hiatus abroad of the Red Stockings and Athletics the New York Mutuals closed the gap on the leaders.

When Boston and Philadelphia embarked on their trip in mid - July, New York stood in third place with a record of 17 - 16, six wins behind the Athletics and thirteen wins behind the Red Stockings. At this time and until 1883 wins determined a team's standing, not winning percentage as in the present day. When the sojourners resumed play on September 10, New York had climbed ahead of the Athletics and stood one victory behind the Red Stockings on the strength of a 12 – 1 streak.

From September 22 to October 9 New York and Boston met three times. In consecutive games in Boston on September 22 and 24 New York's Bobby Mathews beat Boston to put the Mutuals into first place for the first time all season. During the following two weeks the teams moved into a deadlock at the top spot. In a marquee Friday afternoon matchup on October 9 in Brooklyn, where the Mutuals played their home games, Mathews and Boston ace Al Spalding met head to head in yet another contest for first place. Before an overflow crowd of about 4,000 Mathews bested Spalding 4 – 3 to put New York back on top.

New York had established its mastery over Boston by winning all three games remaining between the two teams, but the schedule then turned against the Mutuals. Boston had considerably more games left to play due to the overseas tour and pressed the advantage, finishing 13 – 3 while New York lost four of its final six. In the end the Red Stockings easily outdistanced New York with 52 wins, ten more than the challengers. Harry Wright had his third consecutive NA championship and Boston had vanquished New York in the first pennant race in the, now, famous rivalry between the two cities.

Here are the leaders for offense, defense, and pitching for 1874.

	OFFENSE		DEFENSE
C	Deacon White – 185 – Boston	C	Nat Hicks – 3 – Philadelphia White Stockings
1B	Jim O'Rourke – 204 – Boston	1B	Jim O'Rourke/Joe Start – 2 – Boston/New York
2B	Bill Craver – 189 – Philadelphia White Stockings	2B	Ross Barnes – 4 – Boston
SS	George Wright – 185 – Boston	SS	Dickey Pearce – 3 – Brooklyn
3B	Harry Schafer – 163 – Boston	3B	Jack Burdock – 3 – New York
LF	Ned Cuthbert – 136 – Chicago	LF	Tom York – 4 – Philadelpia White Stockings
RF	Jack Chapman – 103 – Brooklyn	**RF**	**Jack Chapman – 6* - Brooklyn**
CF	Dave Eggler – 162 – Philadelphia White Stockings	CF	Paul Hines – 2 – Chicago
P	Al Spalding – 200 – Boston	P	Al Spalding – 4 – Boston

Multi   Cal McVey – 233 – Boston

As in 1873, Boston dominated offensively, scoring about 10 runs per game and boasting a 320 run differential. Five Boston starters plus the itinerant Cal McVey led their positions in

*Only player who played full-time at the position.

offensive scores. The offensive runner-up, New York, scored about 8 runs per game and only a 124 run differential.

Al Spalding narrowly missed a unique triple crown for the third straight season. The right hander was the best offensive and defensive performer from the pitcher's box but not the best hurler. The future Hall of Famer was also heavily involved in the organization of the goodwill tour to the UK, all at the age of 23.

Best Starting Pitcher – Bobby Mathews – 1.083 – New York

Best Relief Pitcher – John Hatfield – 2.000 – New York

Mathews earned best pitcher for the second consecutive season. The diminutive righty led the league in strikeouts for the third straight year, and by a wide margin. He also beat Boston three times out of three during the pennant chase late in the season.

All in all, 1874 was a good year for the NA. The league showcased the game abroad, featured an exciting pennant race, and crowned a definitive champion. There was cause for optimism for the future of the league.

Hard throwing and hard drinking Cherokee Fisher worked predominantly as a starter in 1874 for Hartford but still logged the most relief innings in the league with 18.33. Relief specialists did not come into vogue until the early part of the 20th century, although their utility was recognized as a strategy in the first years of the National Association.

Relief pitching accounted for 6% of Hartford's innings pitched in 1874. 100 years later, World Series champ Oakland's relievers accounted for 25% of the team's innings and the Dodgers' Mike Marshall threw a record 208.33 relief innings.

1875

Harry Wright's Boston Red Stockings, champions of the previous three seasons, sailed to a fourth consecutive National Association crown in 1875 by their biggest margin yet. What was significant about the 1875 performance was the throttling the team inflicted on the rest of the league, tallying a 71-8 record, the best winning percentage in the history of Big League Baseball as of this writing, .899.

Despite the dominance of Boston and the absence of a pennant race, NA attendance achieved its zenith. However, the attendance totals were deceptive. Furthermore, the league continued to suffer from organizational woes that would significantly contribute to its dissolution after the 1875 season.

Thirteen teams stocked the Association in 1875, the most ever. Unfortunately, six of those teams failed to complete the season or play the semblance of a full schedule. Furthermore, while nearly 350 aggregate games were played by those thirteen teams in 1875, the most ever in the Association's brief history, the actual per game attendance of about 1,200 was, in fact, significantly lower than the per game attendance of 2,660 in the inaugural season of 1871.

The crux of the attendance problem for the NA clubs was the league's open admission policy. The Association continued to accept the application of any team seeking admission into the league, provided the $10 entrance fee was paid. Issues of competitiveness or financial viability were ignored in the application process. While the acceptance into the Association of clubs from Fort Wayne, Elizabeth, Middletown, and Keokuk demonstrated an egalitarian sensibility, the practice did little to endear the new entrants to the big market teams compelled to spend money traveling to those locations for little or no payoff, or of hosting those clubs to small crowds on the few occasions the clubs actually showed up. One should bear in mind that at this time in baseball history teams were dependent on gate receipts to meet expenses.

The western clubs, spearheaded by Chicago, pushed for a more restrictive admission policy after the season, including only one team per city. When Harry Wright acquiesced in this arrangement on behalf of the powerful Boston club, the die was cast and the NA was done.

Of course, no one knew during the course of the season that 1875 would be the NA's last. Here are the league leaders at their respective positions for the season, including best pitcher.

	OFFENSE		DEFENSE
C	Deacon White – 215 – Boston	C	Deacon White – 4 – Boston
1B	Everett Mills – 159 – Hartford	1B	Herman Dehlman – 3 – St. Louis Brown Stockings
2B	**Ross Barnes – 260 – Boston**	2B	Ross Barnes – 3 – Boston
SS	George Wright – 242 – Boston	**SS**	**Davy Force – 5 – Philadelphia Athletics**
3B	Ezra Sutton – 209 – Philadelphia Athletics	3B	Ezra Sutton – 2 - Philadelphia
LF	Andy Leonard – 231 – Boston	LF	Count Gedney/George Hall 1 – NY/Philadelphia Athletics
RF	Bob Addy – 156 - Philadelphia White Stockings	RF	Eddie Booth – 2 – New York
CF	Lip Pike –183 – St. Louis Brown Stockings	CF	Dave Eggler – 4 – Philadelphia Athletics
P	Al Spalding – 187 – Boston	P	Al Spalding – 3 – Boston
Multi	Cal McVey – 258 – Boston		

As in 1874, Boston players dominated the offense. In addition to the above referenced position players, Cal McVey and Jim O'Rourke provided great punch at multiple positions for Harry Wright's Red Stockings.

Best Pitcher – Bobby Mathews – 1.065 – New York

Best Relief Pitcher – TBD

By 1875 some teams were utilizing more than one starting pitcher due to expanding schedules. Additionally, given the absence of relief specialists, some pitchers used exclusively as starters in prior years were now making relief appearances as well. While a breakdown of innings pitched in a starting capacity or a relief capacity is available for some seasons, 1875 is not a season where such splits are available. Consequently, a determination for best relief pitcher for 1875 cannot accurately be made. Bobby Mathews achieved best starting pitcher for the third consecutive season.

So that's it for the National Association, the first effort at an organized professional league. In hindsight the NA's biggest handicap was probably a weak central authority. Besides the ruinous $10 admission threshold, teams felt free to fail to complete schedules, no set schedule was in place, players signed conflicting contracts with different teams, players and umpires enjoyed unfettered access to professional gamblers, ownership actively recruited players while they were engaged with other teams, and players who were suspended or expelled had no trouble getting reinstated regardless of the severity of their malfeasance. NA management committees proved incapable of effectively addressing these issues. Furthermore, the establishment of the National League the following season did not act as a cure-all to these problems. Years, and in some cases, decades would pass before the growing pains suffered by the NA would be resolved.

By virtue of the staying power of the National League, closing in on its 150th anniversary, the NA is generally confined to the dustbin of baseball history. Through ignorance or conscious disregard, the lifetime stats reported for some players sometimes do not include their NA accomplishments. However one wants to address the *bona fides* of the National Association, for the purposes of this book, the NA represented the first Big League in the history of Big League Baseball, and the years 1871 – 1875 are treated as such.

1875 Red Stockings
Best Record in History

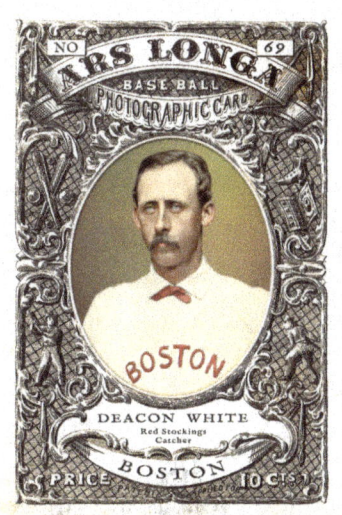

1876

The inaugural season of the National League featured eight teams. These included the strongest clubs from the NA, Boston, New York, Hartford, Philadelphia Athletics, Chicago, and St. Louis Brown Stockings, as well as new teams from Louisville and Cincinnati. The Philadelphia White Stockings (aka Pearls) were excluded from membership due to the one team per city rule. The admission of Cincinnati marked that city's debut in league play since Harry Wright's team of barnstorming professionals was disbanded in 1870. The addition of the 'western' clubs created an east/west balance of four teams each. The National League's most active team in 1876 played 70 games, 16 fewer than the most active team the preceding season in the NA.

On the field Chicago and Hartford battled for the pennant through early July. The week of July 4 Chicago lost two out of three at home to Hartford ace Tommy Bond to leave the teams virtually tied for the top spot. However, following the disappointing series with the Dark Blues, Chicago ran off ten straight wins while Hartford lost six of ten. Chicago's lead was insurmountable from that point and the Windy City had its first pennant.

Chicago had broken Boston's dynastic hold on the pennant, but only by signing away four of the Red Stockings' key players from the record setting 1875 championship club, Ross Barnes, Al Spalding, Cal McVey, and Deacon White. Despite the reform oriented agenda advanced by Chicago owner William Hulbert to justify the break from the NA and the formation of a new league, the four Boston stars were signed during the 1875 season to play for 1876, an abuse common during the NA years. The erstwhile Boston stars were important contributors to Chicago's success, especially Spalding, who won every game during the summer winning streak, and Barnes, who enjoyed an extraordinary season at bat.

Furthermore, again following a common practice in the NA, Philadelphia and New York opted not to undertake their end of season 1876 road trips. This did result in the uncommon action of both teams being expelled from the NL after the conclusion of the season.

Here are the offensive and defensive leaders in the league by position, as well as the best pitcher. As in 1875, no splits are available for starting and relief pitching, so only a best starter is named for 1876. Although runners were stealing bases in 1876, the NL did not record statistics for stolen bases.

	OFFENSE		DEFENSE
C	Deacon White – 191 – Chicago	C	John Clapp – 3 – St. Louis
1B	Cal McVey – 180 – Chicago	1B	Joe Gehrhardt/Herman Dehlman -2- Louisville/St. Louis
2B	**Ross Barnes – 276 – Chicago**	2B	None
SS	John Peters – 184 – Chicago	SS	Davy Force – 4 – Phila/NY
3B	Cap Anson – 189 – Chicago	3B	Cap Anson – 4 – Chicago
LF	George Hall – 161 – Philadelphia	LF	Tom York/Fred Treacey – 2 – Hartford/NY
RF	Dick Higham – 159 – Hartford	RF	Joe Blong – 2 – St. Louis
CF	Paul Hines – 183 – Chicago	CF	Jack Remsen – 4 – Hartford
P	Al Spalding – 158 – Chicago	P	Al Spalding – 4 – Chicago
Multi	Andy Leonard – 133 - Boston		

Chicago nearly swept the best offensive players at each position in 1876. The White Stockings enjoyed a 367 run differential in 1876, an astounding 200 runs better than second best Hartford in a season of only about 70 games.

Ross Barnes deserves special attention in view of his astronomical offensive production in 1876. He led the league in hits, doubles, triples, walks, batting average, on base percentage, slugging percentage, and runs scored. His 276 offensive output score outdistanced the second place performer by 85 points. This output did not represent an aberration for Barnes. Since 1871, the first year of league play, Barnes achieved the highest offensive output score for every year excepting 1874. A measure of Barnes' success at bat was due to his knack for getting the 'fair/foul hit', a ball hit initially in fair territory which bounced into foul territory before reaching a base. By present rules such a batted ball would be called a foul. Nevertheless, under the rules in effect at the time he played, Ross Barnes' offensive output was second to none.

1876

Best Starting Pitcher – George Bradley – 1.101 – St Louis

Best Relief Pitcher – TBD

Al Spalding continued as the best athlete at the pitching position in 1876, the fifth consecutive year he attained both the highest offensive output score and best defensive score. The best pitching score, however, continued to elude him.

The National League's inaugural season was a banner year for Chicago, which won its first championship, but it was a disappointing start for the league. The pennant race was decided by mid-August and the teams in two of the country's most populous cities were expelled after the end of the season. On the plus side, the league showed its willingness to discipline member clubs in a manner unprecedented in the NA.

1876

From 1871 through 1876 Ross Barnes was the best player in organized baseball, excelling at bat and afield, while contributing to 5 pennants in Boston and Chicago.

1877

With the expulsion of New York and Philadelphia from the league after the 1876 season the NL limped along with only six clubs for 1877. Of these remaining clubs, Cincinnati nearly folded during the season, but new ownership kept the team on the field. In the earliest effort of a league club shifting its home city, the Hartfords sought to take advantage of the vacated New York market and opted to play their home games in Brooklyn. The move backfired as the fan base in Hartford was lost and Brooklynites stayed home. With only six teams the league reduced its schedule to about 60 games per team.

Despite these issues 1877 showcased an exciting pennant race between Louisville and Boston.

Louisville played tight defense, featured an offense propelled by the slugging of leftfielder George Hall, and relied exclusively in the pitcher's box on the tireless pitching of iron man Jim Devlin. The durable righty pitched every inning of every game for the Grays in 1877, leading the league in starts, complete games, and innings pitched, with 559.

In Boston, Deacon White had re-joined the club after winning the pennant with Chicago in 1876. His productivity did not suffer with the move back to Boston as he led the league in hits, RBIs, and batting average, while finishing second to teammate 'Orator' Jim O'Rourke in on-base-percentage. O'Rourke also led the circuit in runs scored. Boston also boasted its own iron man in the pitching box, Tommy Bond, who led the league in strikeouts and in wins, with 40.

The teams traded ownership of the top spot through late August. On August 25 Louisville travelled to Boston for a series of three games with a one game lead over the surging home club. Devlin and Bond, the league's best pitchers, faced one another in each game, and, as was their custom, pitched every inning of the three games. When the series ended three days later Boston had vaulted into first place, where they would remain the rest of the season, by virtue of a series sweep. Harry Wright's Boston team had won its fifth pennant in six years and its first NL flag.

After the season an investigation revealed that a number of Louisville players had been complicit with gamblers and had acted deliberately to 'fix' games. Among the conspirators were pitcher Devlin and slugger Hall. The influence of gamblers on ballplayers was nothing new. Gamblers and gambling on games at the ballpark were endemic to baseball even before the emergence of professionalism. In this instance, however, the outcome of the pennant race may have been preordained by gambling interests. To its credit, the NL took unprecedented action, expelling four Louisville players, including Devlin and Hall, for life.

Here are the offensive and defensive leaders by position for 1877, as well as the best starting pitcher. A significant rule change for 1877 rendered the 'fair/foul hit' no longer a hit. To the present day such a batted ball is considered foul. Pitching splits are unavailable for 1877, so a determination for best reliever cannot be made. As in 1876, a statistic for stolen bases was not kept. This would continue until 1886.

	OFFENSE		DEFENSE
C	John Clapp – 137 – St. Louis	C	Pop Snyder/Lew Brown – 2 - Louisville/Boston
1B	Joe Start – 135 – Hartford	1B	Joe Start – 2 - Hartford
2B	George Wright – 146 – Boston	2B	Joe Gerhardt – 2 – Louisville
SS	John Peters – 143 – Chicago	SS	John Peters – 4 – Chicago
3B	Bob Ferguson – 121 – Hartford	3B	Bob Ferguson – 2 – Hartford
LF	Charley Jones – 147 – Cin/Chi	LF	Charley Jones – 2 – Cin/Chi
RF	John Cassidy – 137 – Hartford	RF	Orator Shafer – 2 – Louisville
CF	Bill Crowley – 100 – Louisville	CF	Bill Crowley – 4 – Louisville
P	Cal McVey – 160 – Chicago	P	Tommy Bond – 4 – Boston

Multi   Deacon White – 172 - Boston

It's easy to see why Louisville was so competitive in 1877 as the Grays led in four defensive positions.

Best Pitcher – Tommy Bond – 1.198 – Boston

Best Reliever – TBD

It ought to be noted that Bond narrowly beat the disgraced Devlin for best pitcher honors in 1877. One can only speculate how much better Devlin might have been had he not been involved in 'hippodroming', the 19th century term referring to the 'fixing' of games.

It was a tough year for the National League in 1877. Due to its limited number of teams the pool of unemployed yet talented players increased, forcing the league to compete with lesser leagues for fan interest. Furthermore, a gambling scandal tainted the pennant race, and one club played its home games over one hundred miles from the city it was named for, with disastrous results. Although bold measures were being taken to discipline teams and players in an unprecedented manner, the fan on the street would have been skeptical as to the future success of the league.

James 'Deacon' White of Boston, who played on his 5th consecutive pennant winner in 1877, and was that season's best offensive player. Looking more like a parson than an athlete, he played twenty seasons, revolutionized the position of catcher, and was selected for the Hall of Fame in 2013.

Boston's Tommy Bond, the best pitcher of 1877. The hard-throwing righty led the league in strikeouts with 170 and wins with 40 while hurling Boston to its 5th pennant in 7 seasons.

1878

The National League found itself scrambling for new teams after 1877. The Hartford club folded after the failed change of home field to Brooklyn. The Louisville club folded after the lifetime suspensions issued to three of its star players. The St. Louis club folded due to financial problems. This reduced the NL, which started with eight teams in 1876, to only three teams, Boston, Chicago, and Cincinnati. League President William Hulbert turned to the strongest competing leagues for new blood and enticed clubs from Indianapolis, Providence, and Milwaukee to join the NL ranks for 1878. The team playing the most games played 63 in 1878, still considerably fewer than the 86 posted by the most prolific team in the National Association in 1875.

On the field, Boston pulled away from the pack in August and withstood a September charge by Cincinnati to win a sixth pennant in eight seasons. Noteworthy about the 1878 championship club was the dearth of offense and of substitute players. In the six team league three teams scored more runs than Boston but no team surrendered fewer. More remarkably, Harry Wright used only one substitute the entire season, and that player appeared in only two games.

Here are the leaders on offense, defense, and pitching for 1878. As in 1877, no pitching splits are available with which to differentiate performance as a pitcher in a starting capacity from performance by that pitcher in a relief capacity. However, the most games anyone pitched as a reliever was four, so it's something of a moot point. On the offensive side, no statistic for stolen bases was recorded, although bases continued to be stolen.

	OFFENSE		DEFENSE
C	Lew Brown – 142 – Providence	C	Pop Snyder/Deacon White – 2 – Boston/Cincinnati
1B	Joe Start – 149 – Chicago	1B	Chub Sullivan – 3 – Cincinnati
2B	Joe Gerhardt – 127 – Cincinnati	**2B**	**Jack Burdock – 5 – Boston**
SS	Bob Ferguson – 145 – Chicago	SS	George Wright – 4 – Boston
3B	Cal McVey – 125 – Cincinnati	3B	Frank Hankinson – 4 – Chicago

LF	Tom York/Charley Jones – 143 – Providence/Cincinnati	LF	None
RF	Dick Higham – 148 – Providence	RF	Orator Shafer – 3 – Indianapolis
CF	Paul Hines – 151 – Providence	CF	Jack Remsen – 1 – Chicago
P	Terry Larkin – 114 – Chicago	P	Tommy Bond/Jim McCormick 3 – Boston/Indianapolis

Multi   Cap Anson – 159 – Chicago

Boston was very strong up the middle defensively and benefited from the great pitching of Tommy Bond, who started 59 of 60 games and led the league in strikeouts and wins for the second consecutive season. Cincinnati's Cal McVey achieved best offensive player at a fourth position in his career (C, 1B, P, 3B). The other side of the coin reveals that McVey played so many positions because his fielding left something to be desired. Had the Designated Hitter slot existed in the lineup in the 1870s Cal McVey would have been ideally suited for it.

Best Pitcher – Tommy Bond – 1.250 - Boston

Best Reliever – TBD

Bond missed the pitching triple crown of best pitcher, best offensive pitcher, and best defensive pitcher for the second consecutive year by failing to win offense.

With his sixth pennant in eight seasons Harry Wright established baseball's first dynasty with the Boston clubs of 1872 - 1875, and 1877 - 1878. There would be later dynasties boasted by other teams and by other cities in baseball's future, even its near future. However, Wright's was the only dynasty accomplished without the benefit of a supporting farm system, or a reserve clause in player contracts, or a sweetheart arrangement with another team to provide talent when needed. It should also be noted that at this time in baseball history player for player trades were not yet occurring and long term contracts were rare. The Boston dynasty built by Wright was the exclusive product of his ability to discern baseball skill, offer competitive salaries, sign talented players who were immediately ready to play, and mold those players into a cohesive, winning unit. In other words, it was a dynasty formed in a manner never to be seen again.

Although the city of Boston and Boston fans may rightfully claim baseball's first dynasty, historically it is the ancestor of the present day Atlanta Braves. The Boston club remained in the National League, became known as the Braves early in the twentieth century, moved to Milwaukee in 1953, and moved once more, this time to Atlanta, in 1966. The Braves and its predecessors, in fact, are the only club to field a team continuously from 1871 to the present, spanning the history of big league baseball.

Back in 1878, however, the National League was barely hanging on. Problems of franchise viability, which had also plagued the National Association, were persisting. Two of the three new entrants in the NL in 1878 fared poorly and the prospects for success of the six team league appeared dim.

A consistent theme for big league baseball was, nevertheless, established in 1878 which has held true over one hundred years later, great pitching and strong defense can win championships over superior offense.

Harry Wright assembled and managed big league baseball's first dynasty with 6 pennants in 8 season in Boston.

In his 8th pro season 26 year old Adrian 'Cap' Anson was the NL's best offensive performer in 1878 playing all over the field for Chicago.

1878

Tommy Bond put together back-to-back 40 win seasons, again led the league in strikeouts, and started all but one of Boston's 60 games in 1878 on his way to achieving best pitcher for the second consecutive season.

1879

The NL scrambled to avoid extinction after 1878 as club viability continued to plague the league. The Indianapolis and Milwaukee clubs, which had dismal records the previous season, did not return. NL President Hulbert again recruited the most successful teams from rival leagues which netted clubs from Troy, Syracuse, and Buffalo. A fourth club was also added from Cleveland. These additions brought the League back to its 1876 level of eight teams. An ambitious schedule of 85 games was established for the replenished NL.

Fortuitously, 1879 featured the most exciting pennant race since 1871, the first year of organized league play. Boston and Providence contended for the pennant up to the final week of the season.

Providence benefited from the defections of George Wright and 'Orator' Jim O'Rourke from Boston into their own starting lineup. Wright also took the managerial reins. The club's offensive star was Paul Hines, a veteran in his eighth year. Hines would collect the most hits in the league and boast the best batting average, .357. In the pitcher's box the Grays relied on nineteen-year-old righthander John Montgomery Ward, who would lead the league in wins with 47, and veteran Bobby Mathews.

In Boston Harry Wright did not stand still after losing two of his stars. Outfielder Charley Jones was signed from Cincinnati and had a terrific season, leading the league in home runs and runs scored and sharing top RBI honors with rookie teammate John O'Rourke, 'Orator' Jim's brother. Sensational righty Tommy Bond continued to anchor the pitching staff.

As luck would have it, the teams were scheduled to play each other the final six games of the season with Providence three games ahead in the standings. Besides the three game deficit, Boston was also handicapped by the absence of the injured Tommy Bond, their ace righthander. Adding to the drama, Harry Wright would be managing for Boston against brother George, Harry's longtime star shortstop in Boston.

The teams split the first two games in Boston. Providence still led by three games with four remaining. In the third game in Providence the home team built a 6-0 lead after five innings, much to the delight of the sizable throng of 3,000. However, Boston evened the score with three in the seventh and three in the eighth. In the Boston half of the ninth Ezra

Sutton was robbed of a home run by leftfielder Tom York. The score remained 6-6. In the home half of the ninth, after two outs, manager George Wright drew a walk for Providence. Joe Start doubled Wright to third. Up strode Providence star Paul Hines with the winning run standing at third base. Hines delivered, dramatically singling Wright home with the decisive run. The Grays had a 7-6 season clinching victory as their lead was extended to four games with only three left to play. Providence had won its first pennant in a thriller in the 9th inning before the home crowd.

Some tinkering with the pitching rules occurred prior to the beginning of the 1879 season. The pitcher's box was reduced in size, from six feet wide by six feet long to four feet wide by six feet long. The pitcher continued to be permitted to get a running start before delivering the ball, but would no longer be allowed to turn his back on the batter. You may recall that three balls were required for a walk, but that the practice of awarding a base on balls could involve many more errant pitches than three. The rule was now changed to comport with reality and formalized nine balls for a walk. Another rule change allowed the umpire to fine a pitcher for hitting a batter with a pitched ball, but the batsman was still not awarded first base.

Hitters could still call for high or low deliveries, three strikes were still required for a strikeout, and fouls were still not counted as strikes. It should be noted, however, that the long-standing rule allowing a foulout if the foul was caught on one bounce continued to be in effect. In other words, a foul did not have to be caught on a fly to result in an out. Finally, the pitching distance remained forty five feet from the home plate.

Here are the offensive and defensive leaders for each position as well as the best starting pitcher. Once again, no splits are available for pitchers so a determination for best reliever cannot be made. No stats exist for stolen bases for 1879.

	OFFENSE		DEFENSE
C	Deacon White – 173 – Cincinnati	C	Pop Snyder – 3 – Boston
1B	Cal McVey – 182 – Cincinnati	1B	Oscar Walker/Joe Start – 2 – Buffalo/Providence
2B	Mike McGeary – 155 – Providence	2B	Chick Fulmer – 4 – Buffalo

SS	George Wright – 184 – Providence		SS	George Wright – 2 – Providence
3B	Ned Williamson – 165 – Chicago		**3B**	**Ned Williamson – 5 – Chicago**
LF	Charley Jones – 206 – Boston		**LF**	**Charley Jones – 5 – Boston**
RF	Orator Shafer – 145 – Boston		**RF**	**Jake Evans – 5 – Troy**
CF	**Paul Hines – 214 – Providence**		CF	Paul Hines/John O'Rourke – 1 – Providence/Boston
P	John Ward – 168 – Providence		P	Tommy Bond/ Pud Galvin – 3 – Boston/Buffalo

Multi   King Kelly – 199 – Cincinnati

Providence benefited from strong offense at four positions in 1879 as well as from 'Orator' Jim O'Rourke who played a number of positions. The Grays led the league in runs scored, outscoring second place Boston by fifty runs.

Best Pitcher – Will White – 1.163 – Cincinnati

Best Reliever – TBD

Just before the end of the season there was a critical and far reaching development which was aimed at stabilizing the ballclubs. In an effort to control player movement and salary expense the owners agreed that each club could protect or 'reserve' five players from each roster for the next season. These players would be precluded from signing with other teams unless they were traded, sold, or released. Up until this time a player was essentially a free agent once his contract expired and could offer his services to any interested club. This new agreement among the owners would eventually become known as the 'reserve clause' in player contracts and would ultimately be expanded to apply to every player. The 'reserve clause', although initially welcomed by players anxious for job security, resulted in severely reducing their bargaining power, not only with other teams, but also with their own club. The 'reserve clause' persevered for nearly one hundred years until an arbitrator's ruling re-opened the door to player independence in the 1970s. One hundred years.

1879 was a momentous year in the history of big league baseball. President Hulbert aggressively acted to bolster the league by continuing to entice the best teams from competing leagues to join the NL, which simultaneously served to weaken those leagues, re-establishing an eight team league, and expanding the schedule. Furthermore, the unprecedented measure of each team 'reserving' their best personnel for the next season served to stabilize weaker clubs as well as significantly strengthen management's bargaining position with the players.

Mike 'King' Kelly, John Montgomery Ward, and James 'Pud' Galvin are the newest additions to the roster of future Hall of Famers on the leaders' list.

1879

Paul Hines of Providence and dapper looking Charley Jones of Boston, the two best hitters of 1879. Together they led the NL in most offensive categories with Hines achieving best hitter. Hines drove in the winning run in the 9th inning in the pennant-clinching game for Providence to cap off a superb season.

George Wright, the greatest shortstop of the 1870's, who played and managed Providence to its first pennant in 1879.

Tom York played a stellar leftfield in the NA and NL from 1871. His amazing catch in the 9th inning provided the Grays with the chance to clinch the pennant.

1880

The National League merry-go-round of teams continued spinning in 1880 as Worcester replaced Syracuse. In only the fifth year of NL play Worcester became the seventeenth city to host a club, the same number featured by the National Association during its five year existence.

Here they are:

National Association	National League
Philadelphia (3 teams)	Philadelphia
Boston	Boston
Chicago	Chicago
Brooklyn (New York)*	Brooklyn (New York)*
Troy	Troy
Cleveland	Cleveland
Brooklyn (2 teams)	Brooklyn (Hartford)**
Hartford	Hartford
St. Louis (2 teams)	St. Louis
Washington D.C. (2 teams)	Louisville
Fort Wayne	Cincinnati (2 teams)
Rockford	Providence
Baltimore (2 teams)	Indianapolis
Middletown	Milwaukee
Elizabeth	Buffalo
New Haven	Syracuse
Keokuk	Worcester

Clearly the NL was not enjoying any more success with franchise viability than the NA had, although bold and ruthless measures were employed by NL President Hulbert to strengthen the League. Among those measures was his policy of bolstering his own Chicago club at the expense of the league's weaker clubs, often using his position as league President to his

*Although both leagues fielded teams from New York, the New York teams played their games in Brooklyn, at that time an independent city.

**Hartford played its home games in Brooklyn in 1877.

advantage. Hulbert was a popular target for newspapers outside of Chicago and became the first 'big market' baseball figure everyone loved to hate. His justification for the heavy handed use of the league presidency was his belief that what was good for Chicago was good for the League. While this may have been true to an extent, it was probably more certain that his failure to re-establish teams in the major population centers of Philadelphia and New York following their expulsion after the 1876 season had an adverse effect on the league's viability. Although a controversial figure in the history of big league baseball, Hulbert was selected for the Hall of Fame in 1995.

For 1880 the number of balls necessary to draw a walk was reduced from nine to eight. Three strikes continued to be needed for a strikeout, but a new rule requiring the third strike to be caught by the catcher on a fly before the ball hit the ground was put into effect. No further changes were made to the pitching rules, still a four foot by six foot pitching box, pitcher still permitted to get running starts before delivery within the pitching box, pitching distance still forty five feet from the home plate, and hitters still permitted to call for high or low deliveries.

In any event, by 1880 Hulbert's efforts on behalf of the White Stockings were paying dividends as the Chicago club embarked on a championship streak reminiscent of Boston in the 1870s. Chicago coasted to its second pennant in 1880 with a record of 67-17, easily outdistancing second place Providence by fifteen games. Providence played eighty seven games in 1880, the most official games ever by any team.

Before we embark on the yearly listing of our offensive and defensive leaders by position, some clarification on statistics is needed.

Although no stats were being recorded by big league baseball for stolen bases in 1880, bases continued to be stolen. For some stats which were not contemporaneously recorded in the nineteenth century, researchers have been able to go back and review game accounts and box scores to tabulate the numbers after the fact. Notable among these retroactive tabulations are RBIs, which were not officially tabulated by Major League Baseball until 1920. Nevertheless, we have RBI totals for most years because researchers have studied game accounts and box scores which make RBIs relatively easy to figure out. The problem with retroactively counting stolen bases in the same manner has to do with what was considered a stolen base in the nineteenth century. Up until 1898 a runner was credited with a stolen base when a swipe was accomplished in the manner we recognize in the present day, but also when he advanced an extra base on a hit or an out. Perusal of box scores would not be helpful in figuring out how bases were stolen and, thus far, no one has succeeded in reconstructing stolen bases in the modern sense from game accounts, a task which would be truly Herculean in the undertaking. When big league baseball decided to tabulate stolen bases in 1886 no distinction was made as to how they were stolen and, once again, no one has figured it out retroactively. As a consequence of the expansive definition of a stolen base in effect through 1897, stolen base totals from 1886 through 1897 are greatly inflated compared to the present day.

Anyway, stolen bases were not tabulated in 1880 so the offensive scores do not include a stolen base value. Additionally, no splits are available for pitchers so a determination for best relief pitcher could not be made. Here are the leaders.

	OFFENSE		DEFENSE
C	Emil Gross – 130 – Providence	C	John Clapp – 1 – Cincinnati
1B	Cap Anson – 198 – Chicago	1B	Bill Phillips – 2 – Cleveland
2B	Fred Dunlap – 152 – Cleveland	**2B**	**Jack Burdock – 6 – Boston**
SS	Tom Burns – 152 – Chicago	SS	Arthur Irwin – 3 – Worcester
3B	Roger Connor – 166 – Troy	3B	Hick Carpenter/Art Whitney – 1 - Cincinnati/Worcester
LF	**Abner Dalrymple – 203 – Chicago**	LF	Patrick Gillespie – 5 – Troy
RF	King Kelly – 193 – Chicago	**RF**	**Orator Shafer – 6 – Cleveland**
CF	George Gore – 190 – Chicago	CF	Paul Hines – 3 – Providence
P	Curry Foley – 130 – Boston	P	Tommy Bond – 3 – Boston
Multi	Orator O'Rourke – 175 – Boston		

Chicago's offense was simply overwhelming in 1880, scoring over one hundred more runs than the second best offense in Providence, which actually played one additional game.

Best pitcher – Jim McCormick – 1.144 – Cleveland

Best Reliever – TBD

Jim McCormick beat Chicago four times in 1880. No other team, much less any other pitcher, beat Chicago more than three times. Not surprisingly, by 1885 McCormick was pitching *for* Chicago.

Roger Connor is the latest addition to our roster of future Hall of Famers from the leaders' list, which now stands at ten. Connor went on to set the major league career home run record, although unheralded at the time, which he held until 1921 when the record was broken by Babe Ruth.

Abner Dalrymple banged out a league leading 126 hits and scored a remarkable 91 runs in only 86 games for pennant winning Chicago in 1880 on his way to achieving best hitter.

Jim McCormick, pitching for Cleveland in 1880, led the league in innings pitched with 657.67 and wins with 45. The righty also managed to deal mighty Chicago 4 of their 17 losses that season.

NL President Hulbert believed what was good for Chicago was good for the league. Perhaps not coincidentally, he was also majority owner in Chicago.

1881

Cincinnati was expelled from the National League following the 1880 season. The expulsion resulted from the failure of club ownership to agree to adhere to the league's rules concerning no games on Sunday and no sales or consumption of beer/alcohol at games. Cincinnati management wished to continue to reap profits provided by the city's ethnic German community, which was accustomed to attending Sunday games and enjoying sudsy refreshment. This expulsion later contributed to the formation of the rival American Association in 1882, interrupting the NL monopoly on major league baseball.

Detroit replaced Cincinnati in the NL ranks to maintain the number of teams at eight for 1881. Eighty five games per team were scheduled for the season, roughly the same as in 1880.

Since 1877 the league batting average had had been steadily decreasing. Even with the reduction in the number of balls required for a walk which was put into effect for 1880, league batting average and on-base percentage worsened for that season while league ERA for pitchers improved. The NL decided that the decline in offensive production necessitated more drastic tinkering with the pitching rules for 1881. Consequently, for the second consecutive season, the number of balls required to draw a walk was again reduced, from eight to seven. More significantly, the four foot by six foot pitching box was moved five feet further away from the home plate, to fifty feet. This was the first increase in the pitching distance since the inaugural season of organized league play in 1871.

These developments together reduced the pitcher's advantage over the hitter, but that advantage remained considerable. The hurler continued to be permitted to get a running start before delivering the ball from the pitching box. Furthermore, because no more than one or two balls were used in a game, the ball became more difficult for a batter to drive as a game progressed. On the other side of the coin, fielders rarely wore gloves, and batters were still entitled to call for high or low pitches. To put all this in perspective, although league batting average and on-base percentage increased in 1881, no player had ever hit as many as ten home runs in a season in this, the eleventh year of league play. As a result of the 1881 pitching adjustments, league ERA did increase, from 2.37 in 1880, to 2.77. To put those numbers in some context, combined ERA one hundred years later in the American League and National League was 3.58. Playing conditions in 1881 still very much favored the pitcher.

On the field defending champion Chicago was pressed by the Buffalo Bisons for the top spot through the end of July. The Bisons featured a potent lineup with veterans Orator O'Rourke and Deacon White, as well as youngsters Jack Rowe, Hardy Richardson, and Big Dan Brouthers. Brouthers would lead the league in home runs with eight. In the pitcher's box Buffalo relied predominantly on future Hall of Famer James 'Pud' Galvin.

The White Stockings fielded the same powerful lineup from the previous season, with player/manager Cap Anson, Abner Dalrymple, George Gore, and Mike 'King' Kelly propelling the offense. Anson was particularly productive in 1881, leading the league with a .399 batting average as well as in hits and RBIs. Larry Corcoran and Fred Goldsmith shared the pitching duties.

On August 2 Chicago, losers of seven of their last nine, hosted Buffalo for a three game series. Not two weeks earlier Buffalo had swept Chicago in Buffalo, scoring 10, 8, and 11 runs in the three games. This time around, however, the Bison bats were stifled by Goldsmith and Corcoran, who yielded two runs the entire series and concluded their own three game sweep with back to back shutouts. With a seven game lead Chicago was not challenged again and won their second straight pennant.

Here are the leaders on offense and defense for 1881, as well as best pitcher. Once again, no pitching splits are available so a determination for best reliever cannot be made. The absence of any stat for stolen bases continues.

	OFFENSE		DEFENSE
C	Charlie Bennett – 159 – Detroit	C	Charlie Bennett – 3 – Detroit
1B	**Cap Anson – 236 – Chicago**	**1B**	**Cap Anson – 5 – Chicago**
2B	Jack Farrell – 152 – Providence	2B	Joe Quest – 2 – Chicago
SS	Tom Burns/Jack Glasscock – 136 - Chicago/Cleveland	SS	Jack Glasscock – 4 – Cleveland
3B	Ned Williamson – 158 – Chicago	3B	Ned Williamson – 3 – Chicago
LF	Abner Dalrymple – 176 – Chicago	**LF**	**Joe Hornung – 5 – Boston**

RF	King Kelly – 205 – Chicago		RF	Jake Evans – 4 – Troy
CF	George Gore – 192 – Chicago		**CF**	**Hardy Richardson – 5 – Buffalo**
P	John Ward – 162 – Providence		P	Pud Galvin – 3 – Buffalo
Multi	Deacon White – 175 – Buffalo			

As in 1880, Chicago dominated offense, again scoring over one hundred more runs than second best Providence, a staggering amount in just 84 games. Chicago also boasted the least runs allowed in 1881, which they failed to accomplish the previous season.

Best Pitcher – George Derby - .913 - Detroit

Best Reliever – TBD

Although a best reliever could not be determined, it should be noted that not much relieving was occurring at this time, with each team averaging about five relief appearances all season. It was, however, becoming a trend for teams to utilize more than one starting pitcher to pitch a significant number of games. This was an inevitable development in view of the consistently expanded schedule of over 80 games and the increased pitching distance, factors which rendered the use of only one starting pitcher increasingly impractical.

The Chicago dynamo continued to hum in 1881. With the establishment of the reserve system there was every reason to believe that the nucleus of the club would remain intact for the foreseeable future. Despite the offensive achievements of the White Stockings in both 1880 and 1881, however, rules and playing conditions continued to favor the pitcher over the batter.

Pud Galvin appeared as best defender from the pitcher's box for the second time in three seasons. Although climbing onto the leaders' board with his defense, 'Pud' would go on to become a member of the exclusive 300+ victory club.

Big League Baseball: A History | 47

The feisty and mustachioed Chicago outfield of 1881; Gore, centerfield, Kelly, righfield, and Dalrymple, leftfield: first, second, and third in the league in runs scored.

Chicago pitching ace Larry Corcoran, who led the NL with a record of 31-14 in 1881. Note the pitching box, which measured 4 feet by 6 feet, and in which the hurler was permitted to get a running start. Note also the absence of a mitt.

Player/Mgr. Cap Anson of Chicago, who was truly mighty in 1881, leading the NL in batting, .399, hits, 137, and RBIs, 82, all in only 84 games.

1881

1882

There was good news and bad news for the National League in 1882.

For the first time since league play was introduced in 1871, every team which competed the previous season returned to play for the new season. This apparent stability of teams constituted the good news.

The bad news was the formation of a new, rival league in cities frozen out of NL membership. This competing league was christened the American Association. The American Association ought not be confused with the American League, which did not come into existence until the turn of the century.

The Association sprang from seeds of discontent sown by the NL. On the one hand there was bitterness from expelled teams in Cincinnati and Philadelphia. On the other hand, there was dissatisfaction with the NL's tight policy of admission of new teams from cities anxious to become League members. Most of the cities which became affiliated with the AA had fans who had formerly enjoyed a taste of major league baseball with the National League or National Association. Cincinnati newspaperman and club owner O.P. (Opie) Caylor, a critic of NL policies, was instrumental in energizing the membership and formation of the AA.

The AA lasted from 1882 through 1891 and was responsible for reforms and innovations in the administration of big league baseball which were quickly adopted by the NL. Principal among these were the hiring of umpire teams, playing games on Sunday, where permitted by law, lower ticket prices, and the sale of beer and alcohol at games. The latter innovation has earned the AA the derisive sobriquet 'The Beer and Whiskey League' in modern reportage. The NL, after initial reluctance, adopted all these policies in view of the enormous profits and patronage realized by the AA in its first year. These innovations, excepting the low ticket prices, have endured to the present day.

The AA scheduled 80 games among six teams in Baltimore, Louisville, Cincinnati, Philadelphia, St. Louis, and Pittsburgh. On the field Cincinnati dominated the Association and coasted to its first pennant. The Red Stockings were led offensively by left handed third sacker Hick Carpenter, who smacked a league leading 120 hits, and left fielder Joe

Sommer, who scored 82 runs in 80 games. In the pitcher's box righty Will White, the brother of Deacon White, paced the league in wins with 40 and innings pitched with 480.

Upon clinching the AA pennant Opie Caylor, although not an Association official, promptly issued challenges to three clubs in the NL on behalf of pennant winning Cincinnati to participate in post-season exhibition series. The challenges were directed to the first and second place teams in the NL, Chicago and Providence, as well as to Cleveland, the other team playing in the state of Ohio. Although the challenges were not sanctioned by AA management and were proposed in the nature of exhibitions, Caylor's challenge represented the first effort at a World Series like confrontation between the top teams of rival leagues.

The NL scheduled 84 games among its eight clubs. A pennant race evolved between the defending champions in Chicago and the Providence Grays. Chicago's offense continued to be driven by its core run producers from the previous two seasons, Cap Anson, George Gore, Abner Dalrymple, and King Kelly. Larry Corcoran and Fred Goldsmith still shared the pitching duties. In Providence Joe Start and Paul Hines clubbed 117 hits each to pace the offense while the pitching duties were divided between future Hall of Famers Charlie 'Old Hoss' Radbourn, who led the majors in strikeouts, and John Montgomery Ward.

While Chicago completed the season with 55 wins to Providence's 52 to finish in first place, the presence of the AA cast a shadow over the pennant race which shattered the "apparent stability" of the NL and its season.

The AA had already established a team in Philadelphia and was rumored to expand into New York for 1883. NL management realized it could not stand pat while the competing league sought to monopolize two of the most populous cities in the country. As a consequence, in late September while the NL season was still in progress, the league voted to tentatively replace its poorly performing clubs in Troy and Worcester with new clubs in Philadelphia and New York for 1883. However, both Troy and Worcester still had games remaining on their 1882 schedule and there was concern within the league that, in view of their gloomy fates, Troy and Worcester would not complete their schedules. This may not have mattered but for the fact that lowly Worcester had three games remaining with Providence, still hotly engaged in the pennant race. The matter was resolved by an agreement to have Chicago and Providence play a post-season nine game series to determine the pennant winner regardless of who finished the season in first place. As the situation developed, however, Worcester did complete its schedule and there was no need for the nine game championship series, but, in this unprecedented season, Chicago and Providence decided to play the post-season championship series anyway. In the interim, Chicago accepted the challenge to play two post-season exhibitions against the AA champs in Cincinnati.

The establishment of the AA in 1882 was therefore responsible not only for Chicago's two game exhibition series against AA champ Cincinnati but also Chicago's subsequent nine game series against Providence. Both of these series constitute the first clumsy efforts at determining a post-season champion. Both series deserve some attention.

Whether as a consequence of hubris or preparation for the Providence series, Chicago manager Anson chose not to play star King Kelly in the games against Cincinnati. One can only imagine the feeling of desperate chagrin Anson must have been feeling in the 9th inning of the first game when he found himself batting with one out and two runners on base on the short end of a 4–0 score. Then occurred the first great moment in the history of post-season championship play. Anson hit a flyball caught by centerfielder Jimmy Maculler. Abner Dalrymple, the runner at third, no doubt influenced by years of glorious victories for Chicago, boldly took off for home after the catch. Maculler's throw was true. Dalrymple was out. Cincinnati had shut out the haughty, twice defending, and putative NL champs at home on a game ending double play! It was no matter that Chicago rebounded and won the second game. The AA had now made its point on the field as well as in the financial ledgers. Its elite could compete with the elite of the NL.

The subsequent Chicago series against Providence also did not lack for drama, but of a distinctly lower order. In sum, it was never clear to the fans if the teams were taking the series seriously. Although management had agreed to treat the series as one for the league championship, manager Anson sent a conflicting message when he started one of his star pitchers, Larry Corcoran, in leftfield and a reserve outfielder, Hugh Nicol, at shortstop in game one in Providence. After Chicago lost game one Anson began playing his regulars but still dropped the next two. By the time the series moved to Chicago the fans seemingly had enough of the championship charade as only 300 showed up in foul weather for a game eight which Chicago had to win. Chicago won game eight and then throttled Providence in the deciding ninth game. Although controversy exists as to whether the post-season series with Providence would, in fact, determine the NL championship, it is certain that Chicago emerged from the regular season with the best record and the post-season series with the most wins. By either reckoning the White Stockings could claim their third consecutive NL pennant.

Here are the league leaders for both leagues by position, starting with the NL. Once again, there are no stats for stolen bases and no splits for pitchers, so a determination for a best reliever could not be made for either league. RBI totals were inconsistently recorded in the AA, so they have not been included in any AA offensive evaluations. The absence of RBIs in the AA evaluations results in lower offensive totals compared to the NL.

NATIONAL LEAGUE

	OFFENSE		DEFENSE
C	Charlie Bennett – 153 – Detroit	C	Charlie Bennett – 2 – Detroit
1B	**Cap Anson – 232 – Chicago**	1B	Joe Start/Dan Brouthers – 4 – Providence/Buffalo
2B	Hardy Richardson – 175 – Buffalo	2B	Fred Dunlap – 4 – Cleveland
SS	Jack Glasscock – 175 – Cleveland	SS	Jack Glasscock – 4 – Cleveland
3B	Ned Williamson – 186 – Chicago	3B	Ned Williamson – 3 – Chicago
LF	Abner Dalrymple – 201 – Chicago	**LF**	**Joe Hornung – 5 – Boston**
RF	Curry Foley – 158 – Buffalo	**RF**	**Jake Evans – 5 – Worcester**
CF	George Gore – 217 – Chicago	CF	Ned Hanlon – 4 – Detroit
P	Jim Whitney – 154 – Boston	P	Jim McCormick/George Bradley - 2 - Cleveland/Cleveland
Multi	King Kelly – 204 – Chicago		

Chicago continued its offensive dominance in 1882, outscoring the second best team by over one hundred runs, while also yielding the fewest runs for the second consecutive season.

Best Pitcher – Jim McCormick - .931 – Cleveland

Best Reliever – TBD

AMERICAN ASSOCIATION

	OFFENSE		DEFENSE
C	Pop Snyder – 107 – Cincinnati	C	Pop Snyder – 1 - Cincinnati
1B	Charlie Comiskey – 107 – St. Louis	1B	Charlie Householder – 1 – Baltimore
2B	Bid McPhee – 92 – Cincinnati	2B	Bid McPhee – 3 – Cincinnati
SS	Bill Gleason – 124 – St. Louis	SS	Bill Gleason – 3 – St. Louis
3B	Hick Carpenter – 151 – Cincinnati	3B	None
LF	Joe Sommer – 148 – Cincinnati	LF	Joe Sommer – 1 – Cincinnati
RF	Harry Wheeler – 116 – Cincinnati	RF	Chicken Wolf – 2 – Louisville
CF	Oscar Walker – 99 – St Louis	CF	Oscar Walker – 2 – St. Louis
P	Guy Hecker – 119 – Louisville	P	Tony Mullane/Will White – 4 – Louisville/Cincinnati

Multi Ed Swartwood – 159 – Pittsburgh

Like Chicago in the NL, Cincinnati also led the league in offense and defense. The defense was particularly impressive, yielding a minuscule 3.4 runs per game, one full run better than second best Louisville.

Best Pitcher – Tony Mullane - .858 – Louisville

Best Reliever - TBD

So that's it for 1882, a landmark year for big league baseball. A new, successful major league was established with breakthrough innovations, a pennant race in the NL, and the first awkward efforts at post-season championship play. Four new future Hall of Famers made appearances on the leaders' board, Bid McPhee, Charlie Comiskey, Ned Hanlon, and Big Dan Brouthers. Big league baseball, now in fourteen cities, was bursting into popularity.

Three principals from the 1882 Cincinnati Red Stockings, first champions of the upstart American Association. Warren 'Hick' Carpenter, a left-handed third baseman who enjoyed eleven full seasons in the bigs, mostly with Cincinnati at the hot corner. John 'Bid' McPhee, stellar second baseman and the only full-fledged AA player to be selected for the Hall of Fame. And Jimmy 'Little Mac' Macullar, a strong armed lefty thrower who patrolled centerfield for the Red Stockings that season.

Each figured prominently in the post-season exhibition against Cap Anson's mighty White Stockings on October 6, 1882 in Cincinnati. Carpenter started the one-out rally in the 6th with a single and scored what would be the winning run. McPhee tripled home two runs later in the inning. Macullar cut down speedy Abner Dalrymple at home with a brilliant throw from centerfield to end the game. Note Carpenter's mittless mitts and the square home plate in McPhee's batter's box.

1883

Seeking to capitalize on their fabulously successful inaugural year, the American Association expanded into Columbus and, significantly, New York for 1883. The National League, recognizing the need to keep pace with the competition, expanded into New York and Philadelphia while jettisoning their financially challenged clubs in Troy and Worcester. These actions marked the return of New York and Philadelphia to the ranks of the National League since their expulsion at the conclusion of the 1876 season and established franchises from each league in those cities. In a shrewd business maneuver, which would later have significant repercussions, the New York clubs in each league were owned by the same management group. Both leagues, now standing at eight teams each, sought to capitalize even further on the game's explosive popularity by expanding their schedules for 1883, the AA to 98 games, and the NL to 100.

On the field, fans in both leagues were treated to exciting pennant races.

In the AA, Philadelphia and St. Louis battled for the pennant. Philadelphia's offense relied on their powerful first sacker, Harry Stovey, who set a big league season record for home runs with fourteen, and on shortstop Mike Moynahan. Veterans Bobby Mathews and George Bradley manned the pitching box, combining to go 46 - 20. For St. Louis, Tony Mullane and George 'Jumbo' McGinnis enjoyed stellar pitching seasons while first baseman Charlie Comiskey and shortstop Bill Gleason sparked the offense. The teams jockeyed back and forth into first place until September when Philadelphia won five of seven from St. Louis to open up a three and a half game lead. Nonetheless, the Browns still had hope for a longshot. If St. Louis could win its last three against lowly Pittsburgh and Philadelphia dropped its final four versus Louisville the teams would be tied.

On September 26 St. Louis drubbed Pittsburgh 20 – 3 while Philadelphia lost in Louisville. The lead was down to two and a half games. The next day St. Louis won again behind Mullane while the Athletics again lost. The lead was cut to one and a half games. On September 28 St. Louis was idle. Philadelphia was still in Louisville and had to lose to keep the Browns' hope for a share of the pennant alive. After six innings the Athletics were in control with a 5 – 2 lead. Then, in the Louisville half of the seventh, the Eclipse rallied for four runs to take a 6 – 5 lead on clutch hits by Chicken Wolf and Guy Hecker. In the eighth Louisville stumbled and allowed the Athletics to tie the score with an unearned run, Fred Corey driving home Mike Moynahan. Neither team scored in the ninth and the game was forced into extra innings. With a loss the Athletics' lead over St. Louis would be reduced to one game with only one contest remaining for each team. In the Philadelphia tenth Harry Stovey walked and moved to second on a passed ball. Lon Knight singled Stovey to third. Mike Moynahan then singled Stovey home with the winning run. Philadelphia had the game and its first pennant for the City of Brotherly Love since big league baseball's inaugural year of 1871.

In the NL a four team race evolved between Boston, Providence, Cleveland, and defending champion Chicago.

On September 1 one game separated all four teams in the standings, with Cleveland on top. Starting on September 8 Boston went on a tear, winning eight in a row, including four over Chicago. Following their debacle in Boston the White Stockings travelled to Providence, now managed by Harry Wright, and provided Boston yet another boost by taking two out of three from the Grays. By September 19 Boston had crept ahead of the pack with a two and a half game lead. Within the final week Providence took two of three from Cleveland while Boston kept winning. By September 26 only Providence had a shot at catching the Beaneaters. Boston would have to lose their last three against Cleveland while Providence needed to sweep three from Buffalo. The Beaneaters dashed the hopes of Providence by winning out and claiming their seventh pennant.

Boston's 1883 champions featured some holdovers from the 1878 championship club including first baseman 'Honest' John Morrill, who had taken over the managerial reins, second baseman Jack Burdock, who enjoyed his finest offensive season, and longtime star Ezra Sutton at third base. As for newcomers, 'Grasshopper' Jim Whitney and Charlie Buffinton had taken over the pitching duties and young leftfielder Joe Hornung led the league in runs scored.

At the conclusion of the regular season it was anticipated that another interleague exhibition championship series would take place. However, the AA champ Athletics did poorly in a number of exhibitions against NL teams and a championship series was never scheduled.

Here are the leaders on offense and defense by position for each league. Once again, no stat was kept for stolen bases in either league and RBIs were not recorded uniformly in the AA. Consequently, for the sake of consistency, I have not included RBI totals in my tabulation of AA offensive scores. Hitter strikeouts are also not available for the AA. Keep in mind that due to the absence of RBI totals in the AA the NL offensive scores appear greater than the AA offensive scores.

NATIONAL LEAGUE

	OFFENSE		DEFENSE
C	Charlie Bennett – 175 - Detroit	C	Barney Gilligan – 3 – Providence
1B	**Dan Brouthers – 273 – Buffalo**	1B	Cap Anson – 3 – Chicago
2B	Jack Burdock – 239 – Boston	2B	Jack Farrell – 3 – Providence
SS	Tom Burns – 204 – Chicago	SS	Jack Glasscock – 3 – Cleveland
3B	Ezra Sutton – 251 – Boston	3B	Jerry Denny – 3 – Providence
LF	Joe Hornung – 235 – Boston	LF	George Wood – 2 – Detroit
RF	King Kelly – 215 – Chicago	RF	Orator Shafer – 2 – Buffalo
CF	George Gore – 236 – Chicago	CF	Ned Hanlon/George Gore – 3 – Detroit/Chicago
P	Jim Whitney – 198 – Boston	P	Dupee Shaw – 3 – Detroit
Multi	Orator O'Rourke – 218 – Buffalo		

Boston and Chicago dominated the offense in the NL in 1883 with Boston getting big production from old timers Burdock and Sutton, who had both been around the majors from the earliest days of the National Association. Ultimately the difference between heavy hitting Boston in first place and heavy hitting Chicago in second place was Boston pitcher 'Grasshopper' Jim Whitney who led the league in strikeouts with 345 and boasted the best strikeouts to walks ratio in the majors.

Best Pitcher – Jim Whitney – 1.187 – Boston

Best Reliever - TBD

Once again, there was not much relief pitching going on in 1883. What was occurring, albeit gradually, was the phasing out of the 'iron man', the pitcher who could throw, typically, more than half his team's innings in a season. This was an inevitable result of the lengthier schedules played by both leagues, from 84 to 100 games in the NL from 1882 to 1883 and 80 to 98 games in the AA from 1882 to 1883.

AMERICAN ASSOCIATION

	OFFENSE		DEFENSE
C	Rudy Kemmler/Bill Holbert – 70 - Columbus/New York	C	Bill Holbert – 4 – New York
1B	**Harry Stovey – 186 – Philadelphia**	1B	Charlie Comiskey – 4 – St. Louis
2B	Pop Smith – 152 – Columbus	**2B**	**Bid McPhee – 5 – Cincinnati**
SS	Mike Moynahan – 170 – Philadelphia	SS	John Richmond – 4 – Columbus
3B	Hick Carpenter – 172 – Cincinnati	**3B**	**Joe Battin – 5 – Pittsburgh**
LF	Mike Mansell – 158 – Pittsburgh	LF	Mike Mansell – 4 – Pittsburgh
RF	Lon Knight – 166 – Philadelphia	RF	Chicken Wolf/Hugh Nicol – 3 – Louisville/St. Louis
CF	Charley Jones – 155 – Cincinnati	CF	Fred Mann – 2 - Columbus
P	Guy Hecker – 115 – Louisville	P	Guy Hecker – 3 – Louisville
Multi	Ed Swartwood – 174 – Pittsburgh		

Philadelphia scored the most runs in the majors in 1883, even outscoring the powerful Chicago offense in the NL. The Athletics desperately needed those runs as three AA teams allowed fewer runs than Philadelphia. As previously noted, I have not included RBI totals in determining the AA offensive leaders for the sake of consistency. This does, however, lead to some inequitable results. RBI totals do exist for Harry Stovey of Philadelphia and Long John Reilly of Cincinnati for 1883. Reilly's RBI total put him ahead of Harry Stovey in overall offense. I note this in fairness to John Good Reilly, otherwise confined to the dustbin of baseball history.

Best Pitcher – Tim Keefe – 1.104 – New York

Best Reliever – TBD

The last bit of business conducted in 1883 was a truce between the competing leagues. The AA and NL executed a 'National Agreement' at the conclusion of the season respecting each other's player contracts and reserve lists. Interleague bickering would not be permitted to impede the flow of revenue.

Tim Keefe is our newest future Hall of Famer on the leaders' board.

'Long' John Reilly of Cincinnati, offensive standout in the AA in 1883. .311 BA, 14 triples, 9 HRs, 79 RBIs, 103 runs scored.

'Grasshopper' Jim Whitney, best pitcher in the NL in 1883. With the Boston and Chicago offenses running neck and neck, Whitney proved to be the difference for Boston with a record of 37-21 and the best strikeouts to walks ratio in the majors.

1884

The harmony achieved by the NL and AA at the conclusion of the 1883 season through the National Agreement was quickly disrupted. A rival, third league was founded in time for the 1884 season, the Union Association.

The UA did not employ a reserve clause in its player contracts and did not recognize the reserve lists of the NL or AA. Consequently, players not already under contract in the NL or AA were considered fair game to be lured onto UA rosters. The establishment of the UA and its roster raiding formula for stocking its clubs guaranteed that inter-league hostility would persist into 1884.

The UA lasted for only one season. A moving force behind the UA was a wealthy fan from St. Louis, Henry Lucas, the owner of the UA St. Louis Maroons. Lucas was successful in building a powerful team in St. Louis but was unable or unwilling to prop up the rest of the league. Most of the clubs in the UA either folded before the end of the season or were not competitive. In fact, the competitive balance in the UA was so egregiously bad (St. Louis won the pennant by twenty one games) that I do not consider it to be a major league. One can debate at great length what constitutes a "major" league, but I believe at least three of four requirements must be met; 1) the league should last more than one season, 2) the league should be competitive, 3) most of the league's member clubs should finish a complete season, and 4) the league must attract some measure of top level talent. Aside from signing a few star quality players, the UA is found deficient in all other respects. As a consequence of the poor composition of the UA I ignore UA player stats and no report on offensive, defensive, or pitching leaders in the UA is provided.

At the beginning of the 1884 season, however, the UA sure looked like a competing major league to the NL and AA. The UA had established clubs in cities with NL and AA teams to compete with at the box office, and had raided NL and AA rosters for players, including some of star caliber. The NL and AA coordinated a strategy to protect their interests. The NL prevailed upon the AA to expand into four new cities as a pre-emptive measure, and both leagues threatened to blacklist players who signed with the UA. Additionally, NL and AA teams were prohibited from engaging in any exhibitions with UA teams. The UA responded by blatantly recruiting NL and AA players during the season who were already playing under contract.

Following the 1884 season Henry Lucas arranged to have his St. Louis club admitted into the NL. The departure of Lucas and his powerful Maroons from the upstart league effectively killed the Union Association.

The NL entered 1884 with the same roster of eight clubs from the previous season. The AA expanded, as previously noted, into four cities, Brooklyn, Indianapolis, Toledo, and Washington, to increase the number of its member clubs to twelve. The Washington club folded in early August and was replaced by a team from Richmond. The addition of Brooklyn to the AA marked that city's return to the ranks of big league baseball since the Hartfords played home games there in 1877. The NL increased its schedule to 112 games, the AA to 108. The teams playing the most games in the UA played 108.

Some significant pitching changes were introduced in 1884. In the NL pitchers were officially permitted to throw overhand, that is to say, with no restriction on the position of the hand when the ball was released. For many years pitchers were required by rule to release the ball below the belt, and, more recently, the shoulder, although in practice most pitchers ignored the rules and routinely utilized a sidearm or even an overhand delivery. The rule was now changed to comport with reality, at least in the NL. Although the AA did not adopt the unfettered overhand delivery the AA did decree that in 1884 any batter hit by a pitch would be awarded first base. The NL did not adopt this rule. Finally, the NL again reduced the number of pitches required for a walk, from seven to six. The AA retained the seven ball walk. The pitching distance remained fifty feet, pitchers continued to be permitted to get a running start in the pitching box before delivering the ball, batters continued to be entitled to call for high or low pitches, and foul balls were still not counted as strikes.

On the field Boston and Providence vied for the NL pennant through the summer. The Providence Grays, on the strength of Charlie 'Old Hoss' Radbourn's incredible sixty wins, pulled away and won their second, and final, NL championship by a considerable margin. Radbourn was supported offensively by veterans Paul Hines and Joe Start as well as by young third baseman Jerry Denny, Hines leading the NL in doubles.

In the AA play was particularly competitive, with seven of the twelve clubs finishing with at least a .570 winning percentage. New York's balanced mix of pitching and offense brought the Metropolitans the pennant by six and one half games over the Columbus Buckeyes. The Mets featured two strong starting pitchers in Jack Lynch and Tim Keefe, each winning thirty seven games. The offense boasted heavy hitting first baseman Dave Orr, who led the AA in hits with 162, RBIs with 112, and a .354 batting average, and Thomas 'Dude' Esterbrook who contributed with 150 hits, 29 doubles, and a .312 batting average while playing every game at third base.

A post-season championship series of three games between the Metropolitans and Grays was scheduled in New York in late October. Because all the "world's championship" games were to be played in New York to maximize gate receipts, the NL was compelled to play by AA pitching rules. Hit batsmen would be awarded first base and seven balls would be required for a walk. The AA restriction on the delivery angle of the pitched ball was waived by agreement of the managers despite Radbourn of Providence being predominantly a sidearm or underhand style hurler.

Ironically, it was Mets pitcher Tim Keefe who was victimized in game 1 by the home team pitching rules. Keefe hit the first two Providence batters, they were awarded first base, and both came around to score. These runs provided Old Hoss Radbourn with all the offense he needed in a 6 – 0 Providence win.

The future Hall of Famers squared off again the next day. In a must-win scenario for New York, Radbourn again beat Keefe in a pitching duel curtailed by darkness after seven innings, 3 – 1.

Providence had clinched the series but game 3 was played anyway before a sparse gathering of onlookers. Radbourn took the ball yet again and yielded only two unearned runs in a Providence rout. Charlie Radbourn's line at series end read 3 wins, 0 losses, 22 innings pitched, 0 earned runs allowed, 16 strikeouts, and 0 walks in three consecutive days. The right hander's performance was a crowning achievement to a truly historic season.

Here are the leaders by position on offense, defense, and pitching for the NL and AA. As previously noted, UA player results are ignored. Bear in mind that stolen bases were not tabulated for either league. In the AA RBIs are inconsistently recorded and batter strikeouts are not reported. Due to the absence of consistent RBI totals in the AA I have not included them for any AA player totals. Hit by pitch totals are included in the AA offensive scores but NL offensive scores will still appear higher than AA offensive scores due to the absence of RBIs from AA player totals. Finally, no relief pitching splits are available.

NATIONAL LEAGUE

	OFFENSE		DEFENSE
C	Barney Gilligan – 130 – Providence	C	None
1B	Cap Anson – 270 – Chicago	1B	Sid Farrar – 3 – Philadelphia
2B	Fred Pfeffer – 245 – Chicago	2B	Fred Pfeffer – 3 – Chicago
SS	Arthur Irwin – 168 – Providence	SS	Davy Force – 2 – Buffalo
3B	Ezra Sutton – 247 – Boston	3B	Joe Mulvey/Ned Williamson -3 – Philadelphia/Chicago
LF	Joe Hornung – 236 – Boston	LF	George Wood – 3 – Detroit
RF	Jack Manning – 181 – Philadelphia	RF	Jim Lillie – 2 – Buffalo
CF	Paul Hines – 217 – Providence	CF	Ned Hanlon – 2 – Detroit
P	Charlie Buffinton – 143 – Boston	P	Larry Corcoran – 4 – Chicago

Multi King Kelly – 289 - Chicago

Chicago's offense bludgeoned the NL in 1884, outscoring pennant winning Providence by one hundred sixty nine runs. A good deal of that offense was attributable to a rules change at Chicago's Lake Front Park which allowed for a home run over the short porch in right field which had previously been scored only a double. Chicago hit a record one hundred forty two home runs in 1884 with four White Stockings hitting more than twenty. Only one non-Chicago player in the rest of the league managed more than ten. Those gaudy offensive numbers, however, were only good for a fourth place finish for Chicago, and a distant fourth place at that.

Best Pitcher – Old Hoss Radbourn – 1.134 – Providence

Best Relief Pitcher – TBD

1884 was a personal triumph for Radbourn. He was the team's iron man during the regular season, pitching through excruciating pain game after game, and achieving a single season record for wins which has endured to the present day. From August 21 through

September 24 Radbourn pitched in twenty two straight games for Providence, compiling a record of 19 – 3 and pitching every inning of every game. He went on to stymie New York in the first World's Championship Series with a brilliant performance.

1884 represented another of those seasons in which superior pitching and defense easily outperformed overwhelming offense. The Grays yielded the fewest runs per game in the majors.

AMERICAN ASSOCIATION

OFFENSE		DEFENSE	
C	None	C	None
1B	**Harry Stovey – 215 – Philadelphia**	1B	Charlie Comiskey – 2 – St. Louis
2B	Bid McPhee – 179 – Cincinnati	2B	Bid McPhee/Joe Gerhardt – 3 – Cincinnati/Louisville
SS	Candy Nelson – 193 – New York	SS	Bill Geer/Tom McLaughlin – 3 – Brooklyn/Louisville
3B	Dude Esterbrook – 195 – New York	3B	Arlie Latham – 3 – St. Louis
LF	Leech Maskrey – 108 – Louisville	LF	Leech Maskrey/Ed Kennedy 1 – Louisville/New York
RF	Steve Brady – 167 – New York	RF	Pop Corkhill – 4 – Cincinnati
CF	Chief Roseman – 175 – New York	CF	Curt Welch – 4 – Toledo
P	Guy Hecker/Tony Mullane – 115 - Louisville/Toledo	P	Guy Hecker – 3 – Louisville
Multi	Charley Jones – 208 – Cincinnati		

The New York Metropolitans coalesced in 1884 to outdistance the unusually competitive clubs in the AA. Cincinnati had a better offense but not as good a defense or pitching. Louisville had better pitching and an excellent defense but not as good an offense. The first pennant in New York's illustrious baseball history would go to the Mets of the American Association.

Best Pitcher – Guy Hecker – 1.162 – Louisville

Best Relief Pitcher – TBD

Arguably, Guy Hecker dominated the AA to a greater extent than Old Hoss Radbourn dominated the NL in 1884. Hecker was every bit his team's iron man, being credited with a win in fifty two of Louisville's sixty eight victories (76%). Radbourn was a winner in sixty of the eighty four wins for Providence (71%). Hecker threw 68% of Louisville's innings. Radbourn threw 66% of Providence's innings. The next closest pitcher to Hecker in the AA was Ed Morris of Columbus with a 1.125 pitching score. The next closest to Radbourn's 1.134 in the NL was Charlie Buffinton of Boston with a 1.121, a much closer margin. Additionally, Hecker was the first pitcher in big league baseball history to accomplish the triple crown of best pitcher, best defensive pitcher, and best offensive pitcher (tied with Mullane) in his league. Unfortunately for Hecker, his Louisville Eclipse finished third and it was Radbourn who had the opportunity to shine in the World's Championship Series.

So that's a wrap for 1884, possibly the most eventful season in the fourteen year history of big league baseball. The season featured three competing leagues, the most regular season games ever, record setting performances from pitchers and home run hitters, and the first officially sanctioned World's Championship Series. Fittingly, Old Hoss Radbourn is our latest future Hall of Famer on the leaders' board.

Guy Hecker of Louisville, who dominated the AA in 1884, leading the loop with 52 wins, 385 strikeouts, and only 56 walks in 670.67 innings. A superb athlete, Hecker was also the best defensive and offensive AA pitcher.

Powerful first baseman Dave Orr, who provided the offense for the city of New York's first pennant in 1884, leading the AA with 162 hits, 112 RBIs, and a .354 batting average.

Charlie Radbourn set the all-time single season record for victories in 1884 with 60 in delivering the pennant for Providence. In 678.67 innings, 'Old Hoss' struck out 441 with a 1.38 ERA. He went on to win all three games against New York in the first World's Championship Series without yielding a single earned run to cap off a phenomenal season.

1885

Although the Union Association lasted only one season, the repercussions of that season impacted the makeup of both the National League and the American Association in 1885.

Henry Lucas, the moving force behind the UA in 1884, accepted the opportunity to join the NL in 1885. His St. Louis Maroons replaced the NL Cleveland club, keeping the NL roster of teams at eight.

In the AA three of the four expansion clubs from 1884 did not return. Additionally, the team established in Columbus in 1883 was, essentially, absorbed by the Pittsburgh club. Hence, the ill-advised expansion of the AA in 1884 to twelve teams at the urging of the NL was negated and the AA reverted to its more manageable eight team lineup. The lone survivor from the 1884 expansion was Brooklyn. Both the AA and NL scheduled 112 games for 1885, roughly the same number as the previous season.

In June of 1885 the AA adopted the NL rules eliminating any restriction on the overhand delivery of pitches as well as eliminating the one bounce rule for foul outs. The pitching distance continued to be fifty feet from the home plate, pitchers continued to be permitted to get running starts within the four foot by six foot pitching box before delivery of the pitch, batters continued to be permitted to call for high or low deliveries, and foul balls were still not counted as strikes.

Another important off-the-field development in 1885 was the formation of the Brotherhood of Professional Baseball Players, a labor union promulgated by NL star John Montgomery Ward. The Brotherhood was formed in response to restrictive management policies concerning player salary caps, the reserve clause, blacklisting of players, and unfair player contracts. The Brotherhood initially kept a low profile, but steadily increased its membership and influence in subsequent years, culminating in the creation of the Players League in 1890.

On the field NL fans were treated to a season-long pennant race between Cap Anson's Chicago White Stockings and the New York Giants.

Chicago had obtained the brilliant young right hander John Clarkson to improve its pitching and in July purchased the contract of its former nemesis, Jim McCormick, to add pitching depth. The White Stockings maintained the same offensive nucleus that had delivered three pennants since 1880, namely, King Kelly, George Gore, Abner Dalrymple, and Anson, among others.

The New York club was bolstered during the off season by the acquisition of personnel from the New York Metropolitans of the AA. The acquisitions were facilitated by the absence of any prohibition on multiple team ownership. In substance, the common owners of the NL and AA entries in New York decided that despite the pennant winning performance of the Metropolitans in the AA the previous season, that management interests were better served by fielding a stronger team in the NL. Consequently, Mets manager Jim Mutrie, pitching star and future Hall of Famer Tim Keefe, and third sacker Dude Esterbrook were signed away from the Mets and joined the Giants just prior to the start of the 1885 season. The rise of the Giants in the NL was mirrored by the decline of the Mets in the AA, relegated to seventh place in 1885 after their pennant winning performance the previous year. Common ownership of teams, known as 'syndication', would proliferate to the detriment of big league baseball through the turn of the century.

Keefe and Esterbrook supplemented a formidable Giants team which already featured three future Hall of Famers, Mickey Welch, Roger Connor, and 'Orator' Jim O'Rourke. In 1885 Welch would go on to win forty four games, first baseman Connor would lead the NL in hits and with a .371 batting average, and, in his fourteenth season, the thirty five year old O'Rourke, patrolling centerfield, would lead the league in triples with sixteen.

In a critical late September series the Giants travelled to Chicago for four games trailing the White Stockings in the standings by two games. In a clash of titans McCormick beat Welch twice while Clarkson and Keefe split their two contests, resulting in a four game lead for Chicago with only four games left in the season for each team. The Giants were unable to make up the deficit and the White Stockings had their fourth pennant in six years.

In the AA the St. Louis Browns, managed by first baseman Charlie Comiskey, coasted to an easy pennant, besting second place Cincinnati by sixteen games. The Browns relied offensively on a scrappy, hustling offense led by center fielder Curt Welch and boasted the best one-two pitching punch in the league, Bob Caruthers and Dave Foutz, who combined for seventy three of St. Louis' seventy nine wins. Chicago and St. Louis would meet in the second World's Championship Series.

The World's Series was embroiled in controversy and resulted in a six game draw or a three games to two edge for St. Louis, depending on your perspective.

The controversy centered around game two in St. Louis. After a tie game called on account of darkness in game one, Browns manager Comiskey objected to the umpiring during game two and angry St. Louis fans stormed onto the field. The umpire declared a forfeit in favor of Chicago, giving the White Stockings a one game to zero lead in the Series. The next four games were evenly split, giving Chicago a three games to two lead with one game left to play. According to newspaper reports, Anson and Comiskey then decided to ignore the game two forfeit prior to the beginning of game seven, in all likelihood to increase game seven gate receipts. With the forfeit result erased each team could claim two wins and game seven could then be billed as a contest to decide the world's championship. However, after St. Louis throttled Chicago in game seven, the White Stockings decided to keep the forfeit victory, and denied that any agreement to erase the forfeit ever took place. Significantly, the respective league offices of the NL and AA never weighed in on the issue of the forfeited game. The pro-Chicago press sided with the Anson version of events while the pro-St. Louis press took the opposite view.

In the absence of any decisive action by League or Association officials there has never been an 'official' result of the 1885 World's Championship Series. If you believe the forfeit should count, the result of the Series was a three games to three draw, with one tied game. However, in games played to their conclusion, the result was three wins for St. Louis and only two for Chicago, with one tied game. In fact, the utterances of Cap Anson should have been considered nothing more than opportunistic blarney as the outcome of the forfeited game should have been recognized if it was properly adjudged by the umpire. This infamous Series became the first chapter in the storied baseball rivalry between the cities of Chicago and St. Louis which has persisted to the present day.

At the time the Series bolstered the stature of the AA as being competitive with the NL after the pathetic performance of the AA Metropolitans in the 1884 Series. While the attendance totals for the Series were not impressive, they were still much better than the totals of the previous year. Attendance could have been even greater had three of the seven games not been played at neutral cities, a mistake the organizers of championship series in the 1880's would periodically continue to make. The controversy concerning the forfeit also highlighted the dysfunction of the National Agreement as it pertained to post-season play. The decision to accept or decline the forfeit result should never have been left to the management of the contending clubs.

Here are the leaders on offense and defense for each league. RBI totals are finally available for the AA for 1885 but batter strikeouts are not. This serves to slightly inflate the AA offensive totals as compared to the NL offensive totals. Stats for stolen bases were not kept. No splits are available to determine innings pitched in a relief capacity from innings pitched in a starting capacity.

NATIONAL LEAGUE

	OFFENSE		DEFENSE
C	None	C	None
1B	**Cap Anson – 284 – Chicago**	1B	Roger Connor – 3 – New York
2B	Fred Pfeffer – 215 – Chicago	2B	Fred Pfeffer – 3 – Chicago
SS	Tom Burns – 212 – Chicago	SS	Jack Glasscock – 3 – St. Louis
3B	Ned Williamson – 207 – Chicago	3B	Ezra Sutton/Deacon White – 2 – Boston/Buffalo
LF	Abner Dalrymple – 231 – Chicago	LF	None
RF	Mike Dorgan – 175 – New York	RF	None
CF	George Gore – 254 – Chicago	**CF**	**Jim Fogarty – 5 – Philadelphia**
P	Charlie Ferguson – 121 – Philadelphia	P	Jim McCormick – 3 – Prov/Chi
Multi	King Kelly – 264 – Chicago		

Chicago simply bludgeoned the NL in offense in 1885, scoring over one hundred more runs than second best New York. Anson's crew featured the best offensive performers at nearly every starting position. New York stayed close in the standings until the end of the season with superior defense and strong pitching, but Chicago still had John Clarkson in the pitching box.

Best Pitcher – John Clarkson - .918 – Chicago

Best Reliever – TBD

Clarkson had a stupendous season in 1885, leading the NL with fifty three wins, nine more than second best Mickey Welch, six hundred twenty three innings pitched, over one hundred more than second best Welch, and three hundred eight strikeouts, fifty more than second best Welch.

AMERICAN ASSOCIATION

	OFFENSE		DEFENSE
C	Doc Bushong – 119 – St. Louis	C	**Doc Bushong – 7 – St. Louis***
1B	Dave Orr – 241 – New York	1B	Bill Phillips/Milt Scott – 3 – Brooklyn/Pitt-Det(NL)
2B	Pop Smith/Bid McPhee – 190 - Pittsburgh/Cincinnati	2B	Pop Smith/Bid McPhee – 3 – Pittsburgh/Cincinnati
SS	Frank Fennelly – 240 – Cincinnati	SS	Candy Nelson – 3 – New York
3B	Hick Carpenter – 218 – Cincinnati	3B	Arlie Latham/Frank Hankinson 3 – St. Louis/New York
LF	Charley Jones – 229 – Cincinnati	LF	Joe Sommer – 3 – Baltimore
RF	Tom Brown – 229 - Pittsburgh	RF	Pop Corkhill – 4 – Cincinnati
CF	Pete Browning – 259 – Louisville	CF	**Curt Welch – 6 – St. Louis**
P	Guy Hecker – 133 – Louisville	P	Guy Hecker/Larry McKeon 2 – Louisville/Cincinnati

Multi Henry Larkin – 285 - Philadelphia

*Only full-time player at the position.

St. Louis boasted the best defense in the AA in 1885 to go with strong pitching and an aggressive offense. The Browns proved their dominance of the AA to be no fluke by going toe to toe with NL powerhouse Chicago in the World's Series.

Best Pitcher – Bobby Mathews – 1.126 – Philadelphia

Best Reliever – TBD

Bobby Mathews achieved best pitcher honors for the fourth time, and at the age of thirty three. The diminutive righty was second in the league in strikeouts with two hundred eighty six and boasted the best strikeouts to walks/hit by pitch ratio in the league for pitchers throwing over one hundred innings. Mathews' accomplishment is all the more remarkable in view of the fact that the last time he achieved best pitcher was 1875 at the shorter pitching distance in the National Association.

So that's just about the whole megillah for 1885, another tumultuous year in the saga of the growth of big league baseball. John Clarkson is added to our roster of future Hall of Famers from the leaders' board.

There is one last noteworthy item for 1885, and it deserves more than passing mention. Going back to 1884 the expansion Toledo club in the AA featured two non-white players, the Walker brothers, Moses and Welday. Being the only two Black players in the entire NL and AA, they did not have an easy time with other teams, with their own teammates, or with fans just twenty years after the conclusion of the Civil War. Toledo was dropped from the AA for 1885 but Moses Walker, being a catcher of considerable ability at a time when able catchers were in great demand, never played another game at the big league level. Sometime in 1885, as a consequence of pressure from various stars, notably including Anson of Chicago, without any fanfare, behind closed doors, and with no formal pronouncement, non-whites were banned from the NL and AA. This backroom policy persisted for sixty two years. For those sixty two years White baseball was complacent to present an inferior product to its fans as the best non-white players in the country were not permitted to participate in the NL, the AA, the Players League, the American League, or the Federal League. During this sixty two year period of segregated play big league baseball continued to be played by Blacks, but their participation was confined to the Negro

Leagues and exhibitions with White teams. All personal and team accomplishments in the segregated White leagues during those sixty two years are correspondingly diminished.

In late 2020 Major League Baseball recognized the Negro Leagues as major leagues. In early 2021 the Society for American Baseball Research (SABR) acknowledged various Black baseball leagues as major leagues. As a consequence of these developments, and in view of a statistical database being available for the Negro Major Leagues as recognized by SABR, reports on the Negro Major Leagues, their best players by position, and their post-season championship series will be a part of this history of big league baseball. SABR has recognized the first Negro Major League as commencing in 1920.

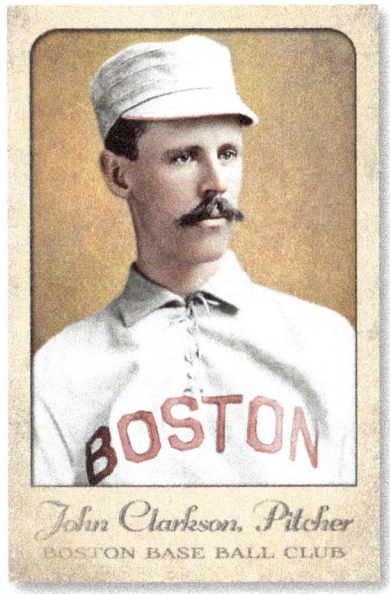

John Clarkson was sensational for Chicago in 1885, leading the majors in wins with 53, innings pitched with 623, and strikeouts with 308. The righthander went on to win over 300 games and was selected for the Hall of Fame in 1963.

Bobby Mathews won Big League Baseball's first game on May 4, 1871 for the Fort Wayne Kekiongas. He starred in the National Association, leading that league in strikeouts three times. He was a vital cog on the staff of the National League champion Providence Grays in 1879. In 1883, from the fifty foot pitching distance, he was the ace on the American Association champion Philadelphia Athletics with 30 wins. In 1885 he finished second in the AA in strikeouts and won 30 games for a third consecutive season. Notwithstanding these many laurels and 297 career wins, the Hall of Fame continues to elude him.

The greatness of Cap Anson will be tainted forever by his boisterous advocacy for the banishment of players of color from Big League Baseball.

1886

The Providence and Buffalo clubs dropped out of the National League at the end of 1885 for financial reasons. They were absorbed by Boston and Detroit, respectively. The vacancies created by the failed clubs were filled by Washington and Kansas City, which kept the NL stocked with eight teams.

In its fifth season, the American Association, for the first time in its existence, returned with the same roster of clubs from the previous year. The AA increased its schedule to about 139 games, the highest ever in the history of organized professional league play. The NL scheduled about 124 games among its member clubs, an increase of about twelve games from the previous season.

Tinkering with the pitching rules continued. The AA adopted the NL policy in reducing the number of balls required for a walk, from seven to six. Both leagues increased the size of the pitcher's box, from four feet wide by six feet long to four feet wide by seven feet long. This change effectively gave the pitcher yet more room to rev up before delivering the pitch, increasing his advantage over the hitter, still only fifty feet distant.

In the NL a season long pennant race ensued between defending champion Chicago and upstart Detroit. Towards the end of the 1885 season the financially strapped Buffalo Bisons were bought by the owners of the Detroit Wolverines. At this time no prohibition existed to prevent one team from taking over the assets of another. By 1886 Buffalo's biggest hitting stars, Hardy Richardson, Big Dan Brouthers, Deacon White, and Jack Rowe, were in the Detroit starting lineup. These additions catapulted Detroit from its habitual domain at or near the bottom of the standings into contenders for the NL top spot. The Wolverines occupied first place into late August but Anson's White Stockings overtook them and hung on to win their fifth pennant in seven years by two and one half games.

In the AA St. Louis coasted to its second consecutive pennant on the strengths of outstanding pitching from Dave Foutz and Bob Caruthers and an aggressive base-stealing offense. Third sacker Arlie Latham personified the Browns' aggressive style with his disruptive heckling of umpires and opponents from the third base coaching area and his daring baserunning, which propelled him to a league best one hundred fifty two runs scored. Second place Pittsburgh stood twelve games back.

The third World's Series would be a rematch of the previous season, but this time for a seven game winner-take-all purse.

In the Series Chicago found itself handicapped by the season long pennant race with Detroit. Although Chicago took over first place in late August, the Wolverines kept up the pressure. Consequently, manager Anson was compelled to trot out his top pitchers game after game to keep the hungry Wolverines at bay. By the time of the World's Series hurler Flynn was out with a sore arm and a tired Jim McCormick was ineffective in his only Series start.

With the Series tied at two games apiece Anson found that he had no starting pitcher for game 5, John Clarkson having started games 3 and 4 on consecutive days. Anson turned to shortstop Ned Williamson and utilityman Jimmy Ryan to pitch game 5. They were shelled in a 10 – 3 St. Louis victory. Clarkson returned on one day rest for game 6 in St. Louis with the White Stockings facing elimination. Although Chicago held a 3 – 0 lead after six innings, St. Louis rallied in the eighth to tie the score on Arlie Latham's two run triple. The game went into extra innings, Clarkson having yielded three hits and Browns starter Bob Caruthers six.

In the bottom of the tenth Browns centerfielder Curt Welch led off with a single. He moved to third via an infield error and a sacrifice. With Welch threatening to steal home, in typical Browns fashion, Chicago catcher King Kelly hunkered close to the ground for the pitch in order to make a play. However, Clarkson's pitch sailed high, too high for the hunkered down Kelly to grab, and Welch scored easily with the Series winning run before the home crowd. The Browns had the game, the Series, the approximate $14,000 purse, and the first (and only) undisputed World's Series Championship for the AA.

This was the third consecutive World's Series. The post-season championship as an institution was catching on as the 1886 Series was well received, with anywhere from six to ten thousand fans attending each game. Curt Welch's decisive run was characterized by the press as the '$15,000 slide' and entered the annals of baseball legend. It also marked the second chapter in the historic Chicago/St. Louis rivalry. The AA could again boast of parity with the NL.

Here are the offensive and defensive leaders by position for each league. Stolen bases return as a statistic and is incorporated into the offensive scores for both leagues along with hit-by-pitch totals for the AA. Batter strikeouts continue to be unavailable for the AA.

It should be noted that the AA schedule was ten to fifteen games longer than the NL schedule which would result in higher offensive totals for AA hitters. No splits are available for pitchers but so little relief pitching was occurring it's a moot point.

NATIONAL LEAGUE

	OFFENSE		DEFENSE
C	None	C	None
1B	**Cap Anson – 369 – Chicago**	1B	Mox McQuery/Dan Brouthers – 2 – Kansas City/Detroit
2B	Fred Pfeffer – 249 – Chicago	2B	Fred Dunlap – 3 – St. Louis/Detroit
SS	Jack Rowe – 255 – Detroit	SS	Jack Glasscock – 4 – St. Louis
3B	Deacon White – 215 – Detroit	**3B**	**Jerry Denny – 5 – St. Louis**
LF	George Wood – 199 – Philadelphia	LF	Jim Lillie – 3 – Kansas City
RF	Sam Thompson – 266 – Detroit	RF	Sam Thompson – 4 – Detroit
CF	George Gore – 306 – Chicago	CF	Dick Johnston – 2 – Boston
P	Ed Daily – 138 – Philadelphia	P	None
Multi	King Kelly – 355 – Chicago		

Chicago and Detroit dominated the offensive categories and outscored the rest of the teams in the league by considerable margins. Cap Anson boasted the best offensive score for the second consecutive season and fifth time overall. Deacon White achieved a top offensive score at a position for the seventh time since 1873.

Best Pitcher: Lady Baldwin - .940 - Detroit

Best Relief Pitcher: TBD

Detroit had Baldwin, Chicago had Clarkson. Detroit benefitted from forty three starts and thirty wins by Pretzels Getzien. Chicago benefitted from forty two starts and thirty one wins from Jim McCormick. Detroit's next prolific starter contributed eleven starts and six wins. Chicago had Jocko Flynn, who contributed twenty nine starts and twenty three wins. In a league with a schedule in excess of one hundred twenty games the deeper pitching staff enjoyed a discernible advantage.

AMERICAN ASSOCIATION

	OFFENSE		DEFENSE
C	Doc Bushong – 143 – St. Louis	**C**	**Doc Bushong – 7 – St. Louis***
1B	Dave Orr – 288 – New York	1B	Dave Orr – 4 – New York
2B	Bid McPhee – 305 – Cincinnati	**2B**	**Bid McPhee – 6 – Cincinnati**
SS	Frank Fennelly – 275 – Cincinnati	SS	Bill White – 2 – Louisville
3B	Arlie Latham – 318 – St. Louis	3B	Frank Hankinson – 4 – New York
LF	**Henry Larkin – 327 – Philadelphia**	LF	Tip O'Neill – 3 – St. Louis
RF	Pop Corkhill – 254 – Cincinnati	RF	Chicken Wolf – 3 – Louisville
CF	Curt Welch – 320 – St. Louis	CF	Curt Welch/Jim McTamany – 3 - St. Louis/Brooklyn
P	Bob Caruthers – 243 – St. Louis	P	Dave Foutz/Tony Mullane – 2 - St. Louis/Cincinnati

Multi   Harry Stovey – 281 – Philadelphia

St. Louis allowed the fewest runs and scored the most in the Association by wide margins. The Browns stole three hundred thirty six bases in 1886, fifty two better than second best Philadelphia.

Best Pitcher: Matt Kilroy – 1.271 – Baltimore

Best Relief Pitcher: TBD

*Only full-time player at the position.

Kilroy, toiling for a dreadful Baltimore club, won twenty nine of his team's forty eight victories and set a season strikeout record which stands to the present day, five hundred thirteen. To put the pitcher's edge over the hitter into perspective, the top seven seasonal strikeout leaders of all time accomplished their mastery in 1884 and 1886.

A second consequence of the extended schedules in each league, in addition to the gradual phasing out of the 'iron man' pitcher, was the increased mortality rate of catchers.

The catcher position evolved hand in glove relative to the changes in pitching. As the speed of pitches increased through the 1870's catchers, who wore no protective equipment beyond, perhaps, fingerless working gloves, were compelled to take their positions well behind the hitter. The buffer of additional space provided some measure of protection from the velocity of the pitched ball as well as from foul tips, which sometimes resulted in serious injury. Deacon White has been credited with involvement in various catching innovations, including the use of fingerless gloves, the development of a mitt and chest protector, and moving closer to the batter with runners on base to deal with would-be base stealers. By the mid 1880's many catchers were wearing gloves, masks, and chest protectors but the dramatic increase in the NL and AA schedules had a withering effect on the ability of catchers to stay healthy enough to play the position.

Consider the following chart illustrating the diminished ability of catchers to play the semblance of a full schedule:

Year	Average No. of Games NL & AA	Teams	Full-time Catchers
1882	81	14	10
1883	98	16	5
1884	112	19	2
1885	111	16	1
1886	132	16	1

Other position players suffered nowhere near the attrition that catchers were suffering. The lone catcher able to play a full-time schedule (at least two thirds of his team's games) in 1885 and 1886 was Doc Bushong of the St. Louis Browns. As protective equipment improved over the decades catcher durability also improved, but the catcher position has remained the most grueling on the diamond.

1886 marked the occasion of Chicago's last nineteenth century pennant. The aggressive policy of, then, owner William Hulbert in the mid 1870's of making Chicago the center of the baseball universe certainly met with success for the Windy City. From 1880 through 1886 the White Stockings won five pennants in seven seasons in establishing Big League Baseball's second dynasty. Chicago's formula in attracting top talent with big money was greatly buttressed by the reserve system which prevented its blue chip players from departing when their contracts expired. Of course, those players still had to produce championships, and the heavy handed on-field management of Cap Anson kept some of the more outsized personalities on the team on top of their game. Following the 1886 season a number of Chicago's stars, including King Kelly and George Gore, were sold to other teams. The White Stockings, the ancestors of today's Cubs, would not taste the post season again for twenty years.

By 1886 the reserve system in each league had been expanded to include most of the roster. You may recall that a 'reserved' player was prohibited from contracting with another team unless traded, sold, or released, severely reducing his bargaining power. Notwithstanding this advantage, management took the additional step of decreeing a salary cap on player contracts just prior to the 1886 season. This capriciousness towards the players in combination with the spirited response of the Brotherhood of Professional Baseball Players would rock the foundations of Big League Baseball as soon as 1890.

Black players were still playing baseball despite being barred from big league play. In fact, 1886 was the first year that a Negro League was established. Independent Black teams had been challenging each other for regional or national championships for many years, but they were not affiliated with any league. In 1886, however, the Southern League of Colored Base Ballists was created. The League operated in a number of states below the Mason-Dixon line from June through August of 1886. There is not much of an archival history for the league so little is known about it, but the Southern League of Colored Base Ballists constituted the first effort at organizing Black teams from different cities.

Sam Thompson is our newest future Hall of Famer on the leaders board.

SOME PRINCIPALS FROM THE 1886 ST. LOUIS BROWNS WORLD'S CHAMPIONS

Curt Welch was baseball's best centerfielder in the mid to late 1880's. His '$15,000 Slide' scored the winning run in the 10th inning of game 6 against Chicago to deliver the World's Championship to the Browns.

Arlie Latham led the AA in runs scored in 1886 with 152 for World's Champ St. Louis. His clutch triple in the 8th inning of game 6 versus Chicago tied the score, allowing the Browns to win in the 10th. He also excelled at heckling opponents.

Player/manager Charlie Comiskey of St. Louis scored the first run during the 8th inning rally against Chicago in game 6 of the 1886 World's Series. He also acted as an effective buffer for his players with tempestuous owner Chris von der Ahe.

Bob Caruthers not only won 30 games for the Browns in 1886, he also led the club in hitting as a sub rightfielder with a .334 average. The righty went the distance in the 10 inning series clincher against Chicago, scattering six hits.

1887

Both the National League and American Association added new teams for 1887, amid controversy.

In the AA the Pittsburgh Alleghenys, second place finishers the previous season, jumped to the NL. In view of this brazen theft of a team by their partners in the National Agreement, it is not clear why the AA continued to honor the pact, or, at the very least, demand some measure of recompense. Following the strong performance of their St. Louis Browns in consecutive World's Championships, the AA was certainly in a position to try to block the defection or even claim a breach of the National Agreement and carry on independently. This was not the first time the AA had allowed itself to be outmaneuvered by the NL. You may recall that the NL persuaded the AA to initiate an unwieldy four team expansion as a pre-emptive measure against the Union Association in 1884 while the NL itself undertook no expansion. Such episodes occurring to the detriment of the AA at the hands of their partners in the National Agreement demonstrated the weakness of AA management. After feeble protestation Cleveland replaced Pittsburgh in the AA ranks to maintain the AA eight team lineup.

After the addition of Pittsburgh the NL took further action, dropping the fledgling Kansas City club as well as the St. Louis Maroons, the last vestige of the Union Association. Indianapolis was added to the NL roster to maintain an eight team lineup there as well. The NL schedule continued to be set at about 124 games. The AA schedule continued to be about ten games longer.

Notwithstanding the Pittsburgh defection the leagues continued to work together and agreed to adopt identical rules, including major revisions to pitching.

In recognition of the inordinate advantage pitchers were enjoying over batters in recent years, sweeping changes were implemented to pitching. The practice of pitchers getting running starts in the pitching box was abolished. Henceforth a pitcher would be permitted no more than one step in his delivery, beginning from the back of the box. The pitching box itself was reduced in size from four feet wide by seven feet long to four feet wide by five and one half feet long. The front line of the pitching box remained fifty feet from the home plate but the pitcher was now compelled to deliver the ball taking only one step from the back line of the box, fifty five feet, six inches away. The NL adopted the AA 'hit batsman awarded first base rule', and the number of balls required for a walk was reduced in both leagues to five. Finally, and most significantly, a strikeout would occur upon the fourth strike. That's right, one, two, three, *four* strikes yer out at the ole ball game. On the hitter's side, batters would no longer be permitted to call for high or low pitches, the strike zone being set from the knees to the shoulders.

Naturally, the result of these changes was a spike in offense in both leagues.

In the NL Detroit followed up its second place finish in 1886 with its first pennant, beating baseball's erstwhile dynastic leaders, Harry Wright, now managing in Philadelphia in second place, and Anson's White Stockings in third. 1887 was a year of offense and no offense in the NL could boast the likes of Big Dan Brouthers and Sam Thompson in the same lineup in Detroit. Thompson led the league in hits, triples, RBIs, and batting average while Brouthers led in runs scored, doubles, and on base percentage.

In the AA it was business as usual for colorful St. Louis owner Chris von der Ahe and his Browns, managed by first sacker Charlie Comiskey. The Browns coasted to their third consecutive pennant by a comfortable margin over second place Cincinnati. Once again, it was a daring, base stealing offense and the strong pitching of Dave Foutz, Bob Caruthers, and nineteen year old newcomer Silver King boosting St. Louis.

It would be Detroit versus St. Louis in the fourth year of the World's Championship Series.

In an effort at cashing in on the increasingly popular postseason championship series, the teams agreed upon a fifteen game marathon to be played in most of the NL and AA cities. Detroit found itself at a disadvantage in the series as Big Dan Brouthers was injured and played in only one game. Despite having one burly hand tied behind its back, the Wolverines easily dispatched the Browns, winning ten of fifteen games and securing their first and only nineteenth century world's championship. Sam Thompson led the attack for Detroit, hitting .362 with two home runs and seven runs batted in while catcher Charlie Bennett led both teams with nine RBIs in thirteen games for the Wolverines. The hopes of a financial windfall were dashed, however, as Detroit won seven of the first nine games thus dampening fan interest in the later contests. The World's Series would never again be scheduled for fifteen games.

Here are the leaders on offense, defense, and pitching for each league. Note that relief pitching splits are not available but, once again, it's something of a moot point as both leagues were averaging only about two relief appearances per pitcher. No batter strikeouts are available for the AA. Hit by pitch totals are now available for both leagues and are incorporated into the hitting and pitching tabulations.

NATIONAL LEAGUE

	OFFENSE		DEFENSE
C	None	C	None
1B	Big Dan Brouthers – 359 – Detroit	1B	Roger Connor/John Morrill – 3 – New York/Boston
2B	Fred Pfeffer – 255 – Chicago	2B	Charley Bassett – 2 – Indianapolis
SS	Jack Rowe – 323 – Detroit	SS	John Ward/Jack Glasscock – 2 – New York/Indianapolis
3B	Billy Nash – 285 – Boston	3B	Jerry Denny – 4 – Indianapolis
LF	George Wood – 254 – Philadelphia	LF	Joe Hornung – 3 – Boston
RF	**Sam Thompson – 390 – Detroit**	RF	Jim Fogarty – 4 – Philadelphia
CF	Jimmy Ryan – 280 – Chicago	**CF**	**Dick Johnston – 5 – Boston**
P	Charlie Ferguson – 218 – Philadelphia	P	John Clarkson – 4 – Chicago
Multi	Hardy Richardson – 307 - Detroit		

Detroit's offensive juggernaut was led by the two best hitters in the league, Thompson and Brouthers. The Wolverines' purchase of the four Buffalo Bison stars at the end of 1885 paid dividends as Brouthers, Jack Rowe, and Hardy Richardson were all strong offensive contributors. Detroit outscored the next best offensive team by seventy seven runs.

Best Pitcher: Jim Whitney - .810 – Washington

Best Relief Pitcher: TBD

Detroit did not place a pitcher in the top five but a clear trend was developing in baseball with regard to the concept of pitching depth. Longer schedules in combination with the more onerous pitching rules were making it increasingly difficult for 'iron men' to carry a team from the pitching box. 1887, in fact, was the first year since the inception of league play in 1871 that no pitcher in either league threw more than one half of his team's total innings. One year earlier Detroit's top two hurlers were not quite enough to carry them over Chicago, which had three regular starters. The lesson was learned. In 1887 Detroit was the only team in the NL to feature five starters who threw over one hundred innings each.

AMERICAN ASSOCIATION

OFFENSE

- C   Kid Baldwin – 166 – Cincinnati
- 1B Charlie Comiskey – 372 – St. Louis
- 2B Bid McPhee – 351 – Cincinnati
- SS Frank Fennelly – 340 – Cincinnati
- 3B Arlie Latham – 395 – St. Louis
- **LF Tip O'Neill – 418 – St. Louis**
- RF Tom Poorman – 314 – Philadelphia
- CF Pete Browning – 412 – Louisville
- P   Dave Foutz – 282 – St. Louis
- Multi   Oyster Burns – 344 - Baltimore

DEFENSE

- **C   Kid Baldwin – 7 – Cincinnati***
- 1B Bill Phillips – 2 – Brooklyn
- **2B Bid McPhee – 5 – Cincinnati**
- SS Bill White – 4 – Louisville
- **3B George Pinkney – 5 – Brooklyn**
- LF Darby O'Brien – 3 – New York
- RF Chicken Wolf – 3 – Louisville
- CF Pop Corkhill – 4 – Cincinnati
- P   Bob Caruthers – 4 – St. Louis

St. Louis steamrolled the rest of the AA in 1887. The Browns enjoyed a three hundred seventy run differential, over two hundred runs better than second best Cincinnati.

Best Pitcher: Toad Ramsey - .799 – Louisville

Best Relief Pitcher: TBD

*Only full-time player at that position

Ramsey, needing four strikes to record a strikeout, led all pitchers in both leagues by inducing one hundred more whiffs than second best John Clarkson.

The changes to the pitching rules did nothing to relieve the punishment being inflicted on catchers. In both leagues only Kid Baldwin in Cincinnati was able to play at least two thirds of his team's games behind the dish.

Notwithstanding a segregation policy having been established in the major leagues, Black ballplayers were still playing on unaffiliated Black teams and in various unsegregated minor leagues. The best Black team of the mid to late 1880's was the Cuban Giants, operating out of Trenton, New Jersey. Among their standout players was pitcher George Stovey, whose services were coveted by White teams in the unsegregated minor leagues. 1887 saw the formation of the second Black league in two years, the League of Colored Baseball Clubs. The League established teams in various northern cities with two of the teams operating out of the major league parks in Pittsburgh and Baltimore. Unfortunately, the marquee attraction Cuban Giants elected not to join the "Colored League" and only a handful of games were played before the organization folded in late May.

One player with Pittsburgh of the League of Colored Baseball Clubs was future Hall of Famer Sol White. White's career would extend into the 1920's as a player, manager, administrator, and owner. 'King Solomon White' lived to see the establishment of the Negro National League in 1920 and managed the NNL's Cleveland Browns in 1924. His most lasting contribution, however, was the publication in 1907 of 'Sol White's Official Baseball Guide', which chronicled the history of Black Baseball to that point. It was Sol White who wrote on behalf of Black ballplayers and sportsmen, as well as, one would hope, some number of Whites, when he stated "…true sport recognizes no color nor clan and it should always be, may the best man win."

The powerful nucleus of the Detroit Wolverines offense in 1887:
Thompson - 118 Runs, 167 RBIs, 62 Extra Base Hits, .372 BA, HOF 1974
Brouthers - 153 Runs, 97 RBIs, 68 Extra Base Hits, .338 BA, HOF 1945

Hall of Famer Sol White, who played for the short-lived 'Colored League' in 1887 and remained a significant presence in Black Baseball through the 1920's as a player, owner, and manager. His 1907 'Official Baseball Guide' chronicled the history of Black Baseball in the 19th century. Note the fencepost-like bat.

1888

Only one franchise dropped away from the big league ranks for 1888, but it was a significant one.

The New York Metropolitans, champions of the AA as recently as 1884, were disbanded at the end of 1887. Following the championship season, you may recall that the joint owners of the AA Metropolitans and NL Giants elected to bolster the Giants by stripping the Mets of two of its star players and its manager and adding them to the NL club. The Mets were never able to recover their winning ways in the wake of that action and the team was sold to the AA Brooklyn club towards the end of 1887. Brooklyn management promptly repeated the star-stripping policy and transferred the Mets' best remaining players, including slugger Dave Orr, to Brooklyn. When Brooklyn could not find a buyer for the talent depleted Metropolitans they were simply disbanded. The practice of ownership interest in multiple teams, which would come to be known as 'syndication', would become more pervasive and pernicious in the 1890's. Kansas City replaced New York in the AA. The AA retained its foothold in the New York City market with the Brooklyn franchise.

The four strikes/yer out rule was abandoned after 1887 as the strikeout rule reverted to three strikes in 1888 for both the AA and NL. A walk would continue to be awarded after five balls. Resumption of the three strikes rule turned out to be devastating for offenses in both leagues. The NL batting average in 1887 was .269. In 1888 it sunk to .239. A comparable dip occurred in the AA, from .273 to .238. 1888 would be a year of the pitcher. Both leagues featured rosters of eight teams playing about 135 games for 1888.

On the field in the NL manager Jim Mutrie's New York Giants coasted to their first pennant, nine games better than second place Chicago. In the year of the pitcher it was New York which boasted the best pitching staff, with thirty five game winner Tim Keefe, twenty six game winner Mickey Welch, and a league leading team ERA of 1.96. Future Hall of Famers Roger Connor and Buck Ewing, along with second baseman Danny Richardson and rightfielder Mike Tiernan, paced the offense. The slugging Connor placed second in the NL in triples and home runs.

In the AA three-time defending champion St. Louis underwent a housecleaning. Following the disappointing showing of the Browns in the 1887 World's Championship Series against

Detroit, volatile owner Chris von der Ahe sent a number of his star players packing. Dave Foutz and Bob Caruthers, anchors of the pitching staff the previous three seasons, were sold to the rejuvenated Brooklyn club. In fact, Brooklyn began collecting all manner of talent across the AA in its drive to unseat the Browns as AA champs. As a consequence, the Browns found themselves in an uncharacteristic season-long pennant race, which also included Philadelphia and Cincinnati.

At the end of play on August 1 St. Louis held first place by one half game over Brooklyn with Cincinnati three games back and Philadelphia in fourth place only four and one half games off the pace. From August 2 through August 12 the Browns played eight consecutive games against Brooklyn and Philadelphia, mostly on the road. At the conclusion of the grueling stretch of games against two of their closest opponents the Browns had won five and lost only one with two games ending in ties. Twenty year old St. Louis ace Silver King earned all five wins and the pretenders to the Browns' pennant dominance faded into the distance. St. Louis ended up winning its fourth consecutive pennant by six and one half games over Brooklyn. In addition to the stellar pitching of Silver King the Browns exhibited a potent lineup. Leftfielder Tip O'Neill led the league in hits while four Browns, player/manager Comiskey, Yank Robinson, future Hall of Famer Tommy McCarthy, and Arlie Latham scored over one hundred runs. Third sacker Latham also continued to tear up the basepaths, stealing one hundred nine to lead the majors.

The Browns would meet the Giants in the fifth World's Championship Series.

In a ten game World's Series with six games at various locations in the east and the final four in St. Louis, the Giants achieved their first World's Championship in their storied history, six games to four. The series was actually more lopsided, however, as St. Louis dropped the first five of six games. The best pitchers in each league, Tim Keefe and Silver King, faced each other three times in the first six games with Keefe prevailing each time. His line for four series games read 4 wins 0 losses, 35 innings, 30 strikeouts, 9 walks and only 2 earned runs on 18 hits allowed. The series represented a personal triumph for Keefe as well as vindication after being dominated by Old Hoss Radbourn in the 1884 series when Keefe was pitching for the AA Metropolitans.

Here are the leaders on offense, defense, and starting pitcher for each league. Once again, relief pitching is not effectively utilized and splits are not available.

NATIONAL LEAGUE

OFFENSE

- C   None
- **1B Big Dan Brouthers – 285 – Detroit**
- 2B Fred Pfeffer – 227 – Chicago
- SS Ned Williamson – 209 – Chicago
- 3B Billy Nash – 227 – Boston
- LF Emmett Seery – 220 – Indianapolis
- RF Mike Tiernan – 204 – New York
- CF Jimmy Ryan – 272 – Chicago
- P   George Van Haltren – 141 – Chicago
- Multi   Buck Ewing – 227 – New York

DEFENSE

- C   None
- 1B John Morrill – 4 – Boston
- 2B Fred Pfeffer – 3 – Chicago
- SS Jack Glasscock – 3 – Indianapolis
- **3B Billy Nash – 5 – Boston**
- LF Emmett Seery – 3 – Indianapolis
- RF Jim Fogarty – 3 – Philadelphia
- CF Billy Sunday – 4 – Pittsburgh
- P   Charlie Buffinton – 3 - Philadelphia

Offensive output diminished significantly with the re-establishment of the three strikes/yer out rule. Five teams in 1887 scored more runs than the best offensive team in the NL in 1888, which played about eight more games.

Best Pitcher – Tim Keefe - .978 - New York

Best Reliever – TBD

The Giants won the pennant with pitching in 1888 and Keefe was baseball's best pitcher. He led the NL in wins and earned run average and the majors in strikeouts and strikeouts versus walks/hit by pitch ratio. The future Hall of Famer went on to stifle the AA's best in the World's Championship Series. The righthander delivered a season for the ages.

AMERICAN ASSOCIATION

	OFFENSE		DEFENSE
C	None	C	None
1B	**Long John Reilly – 317 – Cincinnati**	1B	Bill Phillips – 5 – Kansas City
2B	Lou Bierbauer – 249 – Philadelphia	2B	Bid McPhee – 3 – Cincinnati
SS	Frank Fennelly – 209 – Cinn/Phila	SS	Henry Easterday – 3 – Kansas City
3B	George Pinkney – 287 – Brooklyn	**3B**	**Billy Shindle – 6 – Baltimore**
LF	Harry Stovey – 293 – Philadelphia	LF	Harry Stovey – 3 – Philadelphia
RF	Tommy McCarthy – 278 – St. Louis	RF	Tommy McCarthy – 3 – St. Louis
CF	Curt Welch – 300 – Philadelphia	CF	Pop Corkhill – 2 – Cinn/Bklyn
P	Bob Caruthers – 162 – Brooklyn	P	Tom Sullivan/Mike Mattimore – 2 – Kansas City/Philadelphia

Multi   Hub Collins – 294 – Louisville/Bklyn

The Browns accomplished the best run differential in the majors in 1888, and by a wide margin. Long John Reilly of Cincinnati led the AA in home runs, runs batted in, and slugging percentage in 1888.

Best Pitcher – Silver King – .747 – St. Louis

Best Reliever – TBD

King was a workhorse for the pennant winning Browns in 1888, starting sixty four of their one hundred thirty seven games and leading the majors in games started, innings pitched, earned run average, and wins, with forty five. The Browns' defense supported him with the fewest errors in the circuit. Not surprisingly, St. Louis yielded the fewest runs in the AA.

With their fourth consecutive pennant the St. Louis Browns became big league baseball's third dynasty and the only one to be claimed by the short lived American Association. The accomplishment was rendered all the more remarkable in view of the departure of four key players from 1887 to 1888, pitcher/outfielders Foutz and Caruthers, shortstop Bill Gleason, and the brilliant centerfielder Curt Welch. Mercurial St. Louis owner Chris von der Ahe is generally credited with being more businessman and entrepreneur than baseball man, but his appreciation of talent is certainly under-recognized. It was von der Ahe, after all, who signed and later delivered on-field management of the club to the innovative Charlie Comiskey, von der Ahe who scouted and signed Dave Foutz, and von der Ahe who signed other gifted contributors to the Browns' success, such as Silver King and Yank Robinson. 'Der Boss' was also prone to both praising his well paid players and pressuring them with press criticism and fines when he deemed it appropriate. While such meddling by an owner in the day to day performance of the team is generally considered obnoxious, in this case the team adopted von der Ahe's persona in their style of play, winning pennants with an offense characterized by aggressive base stealing, hustle, grit, and a disregard for the niceties of convention.

When the remains of the AA merged with the NL in 1892 von der Ahe and his Browns went along but by 1899 new management took over and re-named the club the Perfectos. The Perfectos became the Cardinals for 1900 and have been known as such to the present day. Hence, the St. Louis Cardinals began their baseball life as the St. Louis Browns of the American Association and may, together with the baseball mad city of St. Louis, boast ownership of big league baseball's third dynasty.

Not reflected in the boxscores or statistics was a continued and rising undercurrent of labor strife between management and the players. Players felt aggrieved by the ever increasing number of roster spots subject to the reserve clause, up to fourteen per team by 1888, a salary cap, blacklisting of players, and player sales where the player received no financial benefit. More and more players joined the ranks of John Montgomery Ward's Brotherhood of Professional Baseball Players in the hope that their grievances against management would be heard and acted upon.

Tommy McCarthy and Buck Ewing are the newest future Hall of Famers to make the leaders' list.

20 year old Silver King led the AA is starts (64), innings (584.67), ERA (1.63), and wins (45) for pennant-winning St. Louis in 1888.

In the year of the pitcher, Tim Keefe was the best pitcher. The Hall of Famer led the Giants to their first pennant and beat St. Louis four times in the 1888 World's Championship Series.

Often ridiculed in the press for his German accent, von der Ahe's Browns won four consecutive AA pennants from 1885 through 1888 with a tie and a win in four World's Championships against the NL.

1889

For the second consecutive year a recent pennant winner dropped out of the big leagues. The Detroit Wolverines, winners of the 1887 World's Championship Series, were disbanded for financial reasons.

The demise of the Wolverines was the result of NL owners colluding to undermine the financial wherewithal of the club. Detroit, being one of the NL's smaller markets in the pre-automobile era, depended on road gate receipts to offset expenses. When the NL decided to undercut Detroit management's ability to pay its star players by voting to reduce the visiting team's share of gate receipts, the team eventually suffered heavy financial losses and could no longer continue operations. The potential drawing power of the Wolverines at NL ballparks, with Detroit's panoply of star players, seems to have been lost on rival team moguls.

Cleveland jumped from the AA to replace Detroit, the second time in three seasons that an AA team defected to the NL. The shortsightedness of NL management in allowing Detroit to become insolvent, together with the continued undermining of their AA business partners, illustrated the NL's inability to perceive what was best for big league baseball in the longer term. Columbus was added to the AA to fill the vacancy created by the Cleveland departure allowing both leagues to maintain their eight team lineup. The NL played a schedule of about 136 games, the AA about 140.

Following the dramatic dip in offensive performance in 1888, tinkering with pitching continued into 1889. The total of pitches needed for a base on balls was reduced from five to four. After eighteen seasons of organized play big league baseball was finally able to settle on the pitch count it would retain to the present day, four balls for a walk, and one, two, three strikes yer out. Fouls, however, were still not being counted as strikes.

Big league baseball also embarked on its second international tour following the 1888 season. Chicago owner Al Spalding gathered many of his White Stockings and additional all-stars, including Brotherhood of Professional Baseball Players president and New York Giants star John Montgomery Ward, on an excursion to Australia, India, Egypt, and Europe to showcase the American sport. You may recall that Spalding was instrumental as a young pitching star during the 1874 season in helping Boston manager Harry Wright organize baseball's first trip abroad. This time, however, the trip occurred after the season in order not to disrupt League play. During the trip an unexpected subplot developed beyond the games between the White Stockings and the All-Stars. NL owners back in the States elected to take advantage of the absence of Ward and supplemented the existing player salary cap by unilaterally implementing a salary grade system on the players. For many players, affiliated with the Brotherhood or not, this was the last straw. Upon returning home Ward embarked on a second journey, organizing a rival league, the Players League, which would take the field in 1890 in direct competition with the NL and AA.

Notwithstanding these divisive management/labor developments, there was still exciting baseball in 1889 with memorable pennant races in each league and the launching of a classic rivalry in the World's Series.

In the NL defending champion New York was pressed hard all season by Boston. The Giants actually had to play catchup until September when the teams went neck and neck through the final weeks. Boston relied chiefly on the golden right arm of former Chicago ace John Clarkson, who was the pre-eminent pitcher in the NL in 1889. Clarkson was the only pitcher in both leagues to throw more than half his team's innings, not accomplished by anyone since 1886. Former Detroit stars Big Dan Brouthers and Hardy Richardson, together with King Kelly, propelled the Boston offense.

New York had no major defections following their 1888 championship. The Giants boasted a stellar offense with Roger Connor, Danny Richardson, Mike Tiernan, and George Gore all enjoying fabulous years. Tim Keefe and Mickey Welch again anchored the pitching staff.

The teams were separated by percentage points with one game left to play. In the closest finish in the short history of baseball, Clarkson of Boston lost to Pud Galvin in Pittsburgh, while Keefe of New York beat Cleveland. New York had its second consecutive pennant.

In the AA Brooklyn persisted in its quest to unseat perennial champ St. Louis atop the standings. The Browns of von der Ahe and Comiskey continued to intimidate opponents and umpires with all the bully tactics at the disposal of the four time pennant winner. The season highlights devolved into litanies of protests over such issues as games called or not called on account of darkness, forfeits declared by the umpire and then reversed by the league, and controversy over whether the contenders would elect to re-schedule rainouts that could have an impact on the pennant race. These low dramas diverted attention from brilliant performances by the players, including Bob Caruthers, Hub Collins, and Darby O'Brien of Brooklyn and the Browns' Charlie Comiskey and Tip O'Neill. As the season drew to a close Brooklyn found itself ahead of St. Louis and gambled on choosing not to make up its rained-out games. The strategy worked as St. Louis could not make up the deficit. Brooklyn had dethroned St. Louis and the Bridegrooms claimed their first pennant.

It would be Brooklyn, still an independent city, versus New York in the sixth World's Championship Series.

A best six out of eleven game format was agreed upon for the 1889 World's Series. Seeking to improve on recent World's Series debacles, any remaining games after the series was clinched would be dispensed with and no games would be played at neutral sites.

Brooklyn won the first three out of four in tumultuous fashion. In a recurring theme from the 1889 AA regular season, there was much dilly-dallying by the Bridegrooms in games in which they were leading as dusk approached. The strategy paid off in the short term as all three Brooklyn wins were curtailed on account of darkness. Fed up with these delaying tactics, Giants management announced that they would forego the remaining scheduled games given the bad sportsmanship exhibited by their opponents. In order to salvage the series, which drew 16,000+ fans to the second game in Brooklyn, Bridegrooms owner Charles Byrne agreed to move up the starting times of the remaining games to discourage any further on-field procrastination. The Giants were mollified and the series was able to continue.

With the concession on the start time by Brooklyn, the Giants hit their stride. With a win in game five New York closed the gap to three games to two. In game six in New York, Brooklyn's Adonis Terry took a 1 – 0 lead to the bottom of the ninth. After getting two outs Terry delivered two strikes to scrappy John Montgomery Ward. Down to his last strike, Ward singled. With Roger Connor batting Ward promptly stole second, just beating the throw. Ward then proceeded to steal *third*. The unstoppable Brotherhood president finally scored the tying run on Connor's clutch single. The game went to extra innings. Into the Brooklyn tenth New York starter Hank O'Day held the tie. Terry blanked the Giants in the bottom of the tenth. Into the eleventh the Bridegrooms could muster nothing against O'Day who kept the score at 1 – 1. In the bottom of the eleventh Terry yielded a leadoff single to Mike Slattery. After one out Buck Ewing's groundout moved Slattery to second. With two down and the winning run at second base up stepped....Ward. The pesky shortstop tapped a slow roller towards short. Jumbo Davis, playing only his second game at shortstop all season in place of the injured Germany Smith, played the ball poorly and Ward beat the throw. Slattery never stopped running. The speedy outfielder scored from second, and the Giants had come from behind to win game six and tie the series in dramatic fashion before the home crowd in extra innings...in ample daylight.

The loss broke Brooklyn's resolve. The Bridegrooms dropped the next three games, failing to tally more than five hits in each of the remaining contests as the Giants won the series six games to three. New York had its second straight World's Championship and first significant victory against a franchise with whom they would lock horns for the next one hundred plus years. Unexpectedly, second line pitchers Hank O'Day and Cannonball Crane shouldered the load for New York, starting seven games and combining to go 6 – 1 while stalwarts Keefe and Welch were bludgeoned by the Brooklyn offense. The front line pitchers for both teams appeared to have been rendered arm weary by their close pennant races.

Here are the offensive, defensive, and pitching leaders for each league by position. Please note that relief pitching has still not caught on as a pervasive pitching strategy.

NATIONAL LEAGUE

	OFFENSE		DEFENSE
C	Buck Ewing – 264 – New York	**C**	**Buck Ewing – 7 – New York***
1B	**Roger Connor – 338 – New York**	1B	Cap Anson – 4 – Chicago
2B	Danny Richardson – 265 – New York	2B	Fred Pfeffer – 5 – Chicago
SS	Jack Glasscock – 327 – Indianapolis	SS	Jack Glasscock – 5 - Indianapolis
3B	Jerry Denny – 267 – Indianapolis	3B	None
LF	George Van Haltren – 302 – Chicago	LF	Walt Wilmot – 4 – Washington
RF	Hugh Duffy/Mike Tiernan – 324 - Chicago/New York	**RF**	**Jack McGeachey – 6 – Indianapolis**
CF	Jimmy Ryan – 303 – Chicago	CF	Jim Fogarty – 5 – Philadelphia

*Only full time player at the position

P	John Clarkson – 97 – Boston	P	John Clarkson/Old Hoss Radbourn – 3 – Boston/Boston
Multi	Hardy Richardson – 295 – Boston		

New York dominated the NL offensively in 1889, scoring sixty nine more runs than the offensive runner-up, Chicago. In addition to the position leaders referenced on the list, Orator Jim O'Rourke, in his eighteenth season, and John Montgomery Ward also delivered productive seasons for the Giants giving them an offense no team could match.

Best Pitcher : John Clarkson – .609 – Boston

Best Reliever: TBD

That Boston was able to compete for the pennant up to the last day of the season with so much less offensive punch than New York and no real defensive standouts was a resounding tribute to the ability of John Clarkson. Boston yielded the fewest runs in the league by far and Clarkson led the league in starts, innings pitched, strikeouts, and wins, with forty nine. Also a superb athlete, Clarkson was the first NL pitcher to accomplish the triple crown of best pitcher, best offensive pitcher, and best defensive pitcher (tied with teammate Radbourn). 1889 marked the second time Clarkson achieved best pitcher.

AMERICAN ASSOCIATION

	OFFENSE		DEFENSE
C	None	C	None
1B	Tommy Tucker – 326 – Baltimore	1B	Dave Orr – 2 – Columbus
2B	Hub Collins – 314 – Brooklyn	**2B**	**Bid McPhee – 6 – Cincinnati**
SS	Herman Long – 303 – Kansas City	SS	Herman Long/Ollie Beard – 2 – Kansas City/Cincinnati
3B	Denny Lyons – 306 – Philadelphia	3B	Billy Shindle – 3 – Baltimore
LF	**Harry Stovey – 361 – Philadelphia**	LF	Joe Hornung – 5 – Baltimore

RF	Billy Hamilton – 350 – Kansas City	RF	Joe Sommer – 5 – Baltimore
CF	Mike Griffin – 301 – Baltimore	CF	Pop Corkhill – 5 – Brooklyn
P	Tony Mullane – 153 – Cincinnati	P	Parke Swartzel – 3 – Kansas City
Multi	Lefty Marr – 296 – Columbus		

Although Brooklyn had a dearth of leaders in any offensive or defensive categories, they scored the most runs and had the best run differential in the AA, scoring two hundred ninety more runs than they allowed.

Best Pitcher: Mark Baldwin – .563 – Columbus

Best Reliever: TBD

Baldwin was a workhorse for lowly Columbus, leading the loop in starts, innings pitched, and strikeouts. He tallied the most strikeouts in the majors, leading the second place finisher, Clarkson, by eighty four.

So that's it for 1889. The Giants had their second consecutive World's Championship and the dynasty of the St. Louis Browns was finished. Our newest future Hall of Famers on the leaders board are Hugh Duffy and Slidin' Billy Hamilton.

Although baseball continued to mushroom in popularity, labor/management strife was ripping the business apart. While emotions run strong on the topic of labor/management issues, consider for a moment the plight of Chicago star Ned Williamson. Williamson, one of Spalding's White Stockings, participated in the 1888 post-season world tour accompanied by his wife. During the course of a game on a poorly maintained field in Paris, he severely injured his knee. The injury effectively finished his career. He was able to compete only sparingly for Chicago in 1889 and then for a brief spell with the Players League in 1890. Williamson was responsible for his own medical expenses, both in Europe and upon his return home. Additionally, he was docked by Spalding for the missed playing time with Chicago in 1889. Upon Williamson's return to the field in the summer Spalding served him with a bill for expenses incurred by Mrs. Williamson during the world tour. No meaningful recourse to a grievance procedure existed. No pension provisions existed for ex-ballplayers. There is no evidence that Williamson was inebriated or in any way contributed to the injury which ended his performance on the tour and, effectively, his career. Williamson was a vital cog and star player for Spalding on five pennant winners in Chicago, owning the single season home run record until broken by Babe Ruth in the next century. In the context of such conditions and treatment at the hands of management, the Players League was born.

John M. Ward began his career as a pitcher with Providence and was the ace of the pennant-winning staff in 1879 with 47 victories. When his pitching arm went bad he converted to a position player and starred as a shortstop for the Giants. He drove home the winning run in game 6 of the 1889 World's Series and led all regulars in the series with a .417 batting average. While still a player he earned a law degree, served as president of the Brotherhood of Professional Baseball Players, and was the moving force behind the establishment of the Players League in 1890. Subsequent to his baseball career Ward practiced law, suing Major League Baseball on behalf of players on a number of occasions. At only 5'9" he was a giant who transcended the sport. Ward was selected for the Hall of Fame in 1964.

Roger Connor, best hitter in the NL in 1889. Connor drove in the tying run for New York with two out in the bottom of the ninth in game 6 of the 1889 World's Series. The powerful switch hitter held the career mark for home runs until broken by Babe Ruth in 1921.

Hank O'Day, who went 2-0 in the World's Series in 1889, won game 6 with an eleven inning complete game. O'Day later toiled as an umpire until 1927. He was selected for the Hall of Fame as an ump in 2013.

1890

Labor unrest in the big league ranks had been rising since the founding of the National League in 1876. Aggressive team owners such as William Hulbert in Chicago and John Brush of Indianapolis had been trying to govern the salaries, contractual mobility, and behavior of the players with the aims of maximizing profits, stabilizing franchises, and attracting fans to wholesome entertainment. Player reaction to these measures was best typified by NL stars John M. Ward and Tim Keefe, who, through leadership of the Brotherhood of Professional Baseball Players starting in 1885, gave the players a voice in their dealings with management.

The gulf between owner mandated regulation and player dissatisfaction became unbridgeable after the 1888 season when management unilaterally took advantage of Ward's absence from the country on the world baseball tour to institute a salary grading system and salary cap on the players. Ward responded by secretly forming the Players League during the 1889 season ready to begin play in 1890.

The formation of the Players League knocked the baseball world on its ear. NL rosters were ravaged, the League losing over eighty players, including a multitude of stars, to the upstart league. The AA lost fewer players to the Players League, but hardly resembled itself after 1889 due to reorganization of its franchises which resulted from the PL engineered upheaval.

The PL set up shop in eight cities, going toe to toe with NL or AA clubs in New York, Brooklyn, Boston, Chicago, Philadelphia, Pittsburgh, and Cleveland. A franchise was also established in Buffalo.

The NL responded by, once again, undermining its business partners in the AA by accepting the AA clubs in Cincinnati and Brooklyn into the NL ranks. Simultaneously the NL jettisoned its two weakest entries in Washington and Indianapolis to maintain an eight team lineup.

The AA, having been deserted by its pennant winner in Brooklyn as well as by the popular Cincinnati club, also had to suffer the losses of Kansas City and Baltimore from its roster. The Brooklyn team was replaced by a new Brooklyn entry while clubs from Syracuse, Rochester, and Toledo were added to fill out the eight team lineup. The new Brooklyn club was ghastly and was replaced in August by the original Baltimore club. All the leagues scheduled about 135 games.

While the NL and AA were scrambling to meet the threat to their organizations, the effect on fans was also considerable. Suddenly Brooklyn fans found John M. Ward, so recently their World's Series nemesis, to be one of their own. Chicagoans awoke one morning to find a number of their rivals from the St. Louis Browns, including field manager Charlie Comiskey, representing the Chicago PL entry. The NL, furthermore, pressed for games to be scheduled at the same time as PL contests in the same city. As a consequence of this strategy, fans had to decide which ballgame was more deserving of the fan's patronage and spending money.

Among other business innovations, the Players League provided for profit-sharing between players and owners, no reserve clause in player contracts, and a ban on the buying and selling of players. Concerning rules, the PL moved the pitcher's box back one and one half feet. This change, together with a livelier ball, rendered Players League games unusually high scoring affairs. The PL opted not to break the color barrier in place in big league baseball since 1885.

All three leagues suffered financially with the glut of games available for the viewing public. The PL enjoyed the best attendance of the three competing leagues as it possessed the best talent. However, the upstarts were shut out of World's Series participation by their rivals. Furthermore, the NL, spearheaded by Chicago owner Al Spalding, kept the pressure on the newcomers with a spirited campaign against them in the press. At the conclusion of the season Spalding and the NL magnates, despite deep financial losses, were able to employ a 'divide and conquer' strategy with PL owners by excluding Brotherhood representatives from consolidation negotiations. The fledgling PL owners grabbed at the opportunity to limit their losses and abandoned their Brotherhood partners. Ward and his Brotherhood had to concede defeat and the PL folded.

Although the renegade players, for the most part, were welcomed back to their former leagues, players would have to wait for the 1970's before they would have a chance at the fiscal freedom offered by the PL. In what could be described as both a dirty and sloppily played contest, management emerged as a tussled winner over the players in a victory which endured over eighty years.

On the field the first and only PL pennant was won by the Boston Reds, which outdistanced John M. Ward's Brooklyn club by six and one half games. The King Kelly – led Boston team was laden with stars from both the NL and AA, including Big Dan Brouthers, Harry Stovey, and Hardy Richardson, who led the league in home runs and RBIs with one hundred fifty two. In the pitcher's box Old Hoss Radbourn and Ad Gumbert combined for fifty wins from the fifty one foot, six inch pitching distance.

In the NL the 1889 AA champion Brooklyn Bridegrooms were untouched by the roster raiding of the PL due to the foresight of Brooklyn owner Charlie Byrne in re-signing all the principals from his squad at the conclusion of the 1889 season. Consequently, Brooklyn was able to withstand challenges from various talent depleted NL clubs and became the first team to win a pennant in different leagues in consecutive years. The Bridegrooms boasted a strong pitching rotation comprised of Tom Lovett, Adonis Terry, and Bob Caruthers, all of whom threw at least three hundred innings. Brooklyn's offense was buttressed with strong seasons from home run and RBI leader Oyster Burns, run scoring leader Hub Collins, and veteran Dave Foutz. Cap Anson's White Stockings finished six and one half games off the pace in second place.

In the re-organized AA the league was literally turned upside down by the PL uprising. The last place finisher in 1889, Louisville, easily won their first and only pennant with a summertime surge which left them ten games in front of second place Columbus by season's end. Veteran outfielder Chicken Wolf provided the offense with a league leading .363 batting average and one hundred ninety seven hits while Scott Stratton and Red Ehret tallied fifty nine of the Colonel's eighty seven wins.

With the PL snubbed from the World's Championship Series, it would be Brooklyn, now representing the NL, versus Louisville in the seventh consecutive postseason contest between pennant winners of rival leagues.

The teams scheduled a seven game series with the first four in Louisville and the remainder in Brooklyn.

The Bridegrooms won the first two behind Terry and Lovett. Game 3 was declared a tie after darkness precluded further play. Louisville salvaged a game at home with a come from behind victory and stellar pitching by Red Ehret. The series then shifted to Brooklyn with the Bridegrooms holding a 2 – 1 series edge.

The late October weather in Brooklyn was miserable. Two days of rain held up the opening contest, muddied the grounds, and dampened the enthusiasm of the fans. In a city where over 16,000 fans turned out for game 2 against the Giants one year earlier, only 1,000 hearty souls braved chilly temperatures to see Lovett win his second game and give Brooklyn a 3- 1 series lead, needing only one more victory to clinch. Alas, this dyspeptic and rancorous season was capped with a desultory championship as Louisville rallied to win the final two games before an embarrassingly smaller number of patrons. The series concluded in a dissatisfying three – all tie.

Here are the leaders on offense and defense for each of the three leagues as well as the best starting pitcher. Relief pitching was occurring but continued to be an afterthought in strategy. In any event, no relief stats are available beyond mere appearances. Hitter strikeouts are not available in the AA.

PLAYERS LEAGUE

	OFFENSE		DEFENSE
C	Duke Farrell – 240 – Chicago	C	Duke Farrell – 1 – Chicago
1B	Roger Connor/Dan Brouthers – 330 - New York/Boston	**1B**	**Roger Connor – 6 – New York**
2B	Lou Bierbauer – 319 – Brooklyn	2B	Joe Quinn – 5 – Boston
SS	Billy Shindle – 319 – Philadelphia	SS	John Ward – 3 – Brooklyn
3B	Bill Joyce – 297 – Brooklyn	3B	Patsy Tebeau – 3 – Cleveland
LF	Hardy Richardson – 363 – Boston	LF	George Wood – 2 – Philadelphia
RF	**Hugh Duffy – 367 – Chicago**	RF	Hugh Duffy – 4 – Chicago
CF	Tom Brown – 306 – Boston	CF	Mike Griffin – 4 – Philadelphia
P	George Van Haltren – 221 – Brooklyn	P	None
Multi	Jocko Fields – 265 – Pittsburgh		

Boston boasted the best run differential in the league, over one hundred runs better than second best New York. Hardy Richardson, Harry Stovey, Tom Brown, and Big Dan Brouthers all delivered strong offensive seasons for the pennant winning Reds.

Best Pitcher: Harry Staley - .473 – Pittsburgh

Best Relief Pitcher : TBD

The PL was a hitters' league. Besides moving the pitching box back another foot and a half, the league used a livelier ball than the NL and AA. The PL (.274) outhit both the NL (.254) and the AA (.253). The differential of walks and hit batsmen versus strikeouts was also much greater in the PL (1,610) than in the NL (493) and the AA (20). In this context Harry Staley had a terrific season toiling for a bad Pittsburgh club. The righthander led the PL in strikeouts versus walks/hit batsmen differential besting the likes of Tim Keefe, Old Hoss Radbourn, Mark Baldwin, Lady Baldwin, Silver King, and Matt Kilroy.

NATIONAL LEAGUE

	OFFENSE		DEFENSE
C	Jack Clements – 209 – Philadelphia	C	Jack Clements – 2 – Philadelphia
1B	Cap Anson – 304 – Chicago	1B	Dave Foutz – 2 – Brooklyn
2B	**Hub Collins – 327 – Brooklyn**	2B	Bid McPhee – 3 – Cincinnati
SS	Jack Glasscock – 273 – New York	**SS**	**Bob Allen – 5 – Philadelphia**
3B	George Pinkney – 299 – Brooklyn	3B	Will Smalley/Tom Burns – 3 – Cleveland/Chicago
LF	Billy Hamilton – 307 – Philadelphia	LF	Cliff Carroll – 3 – Chicago
RF	Sam Thompson – 315 – Philadelphia	RF	Steve Brodie – 3 – Boston
CF	Walt Wilmot – 306 – Chicago	CF	George Davis/Bug Holliday – 2 Cleveland/Cincinnati
P	Adonis Terry – 193 – Brooklyn	P	None
Multi	Lefty Marr – 263 – Cincinnati		

Brooklyn, with its 1889 pennant winning crew essentially intact, far outscored every team in the NL while yielding the fewest runs. Hub Collins boasted the best offensive score in the NL using his legs. The second sacker led the NL with one hundred forty eight runs scored and finished second in steals with eighty five.

Best Pitcher: Kid Gleason - .603 - Philadelphia

Best Relief Pitcher: TBD

Gleason compiled a .691 winning percentage for Philadelphia with thirty eight wins and seventeen losses while yielding only eight home runs in over five hundred innings pitched.

AMERICAN ASSOCIATION

	OFFENSE		DEFENSE
C	Jack O'Connor – 250 – Columbus	**C**	**Jack O'Connor – 5 – Columbus**
1B	Perry Werden – 303 – Toledo	1B	Mike Lehane – 4 – Columbus
2B	Cupid Childs – 325 – Syracuse	2B	Cupid Childs/Jack Crooks – 2 – Syracuse/Columbus
SS	Shorty Fuller – 269 – St. Louis	SS	Frank Scheibeck – 2 – Toledo
3B	Jimmy Knowles – 263 – Rochester	**3B**	**Charlie Reilly – 5 – Columbus**
LF	Charlie Hamburg – 267 – Louisville	LF	Harry Lyons/Blondie Purcell – 2 – Rochester/Philadelphia
RF	Tommy McCarthy – 340 – St. Louis	RF	Chicken Wolf – 2 – Louisville
CF	Jim McTamany – 296 – Columbus	CF	Curt Welch – 3 – Phila/Baltimore
P	Ed Daily – 230 – Brooklyn/Louisville	P	Sadie McMahon – 4 – Philadelphia/Baltimore

Multi Spud Johnson – 343 – Columbus

Louisville accomplished a complete turnaround from 1889 swinging from a net deficit of four hundred fifty eight runs allowed to leading the league in 1890 with a net surplus of two hundred thirty six runs scored. Chicken Wolf paced the AA in hits and batting average.

Best Pitcher: Sadie McMahon – Philadelphia/Baltimore – .806

Best Relief Pitcher: TBD

The Philadelphia club suffered from gross incompetence in its front office and could no longer pay its players late in the season. Consequently, many of the players, including McMahon, finished the season with other clubs. McMahon led the league in most categories, including wins, with thirty six, strikeouts, and innings pitched, despite moving to a poor Baltimore club for twelve appearances.

While no Black leagues were operating in 1890, the Cuban Giants, the premier Black team of the era, remained active in the integrated minors. From 1889 through 1891 the Cuban Giants distinguished themselves against White and integrated minor league clubs in various minor leagues. In 1889 the Cuban Giants, led by Hall of Fame second baseman Frank Grant, narrowly lost the pennant while recording a record of 55 – 17. In 1890, operating out of York, Pennsylvania, the Cuban Giants outclassed the opposition to the point that their closest rival jumped to another league. Although their league folded following this defection, the Cuban Giants continued operations as a barnstorming club. Despite the existence of three major leagues in 1890, no members of the Cuban Giants were invited to play in the ranks of big league baseball.

1890 was, arguably, the most historically significant season in the annals of big league baseball. Ironically, its significance stemmed not from what happened, but from what didn't happen. What failed to pass was the endurance of the Players League, because the PL, in fact, succeeded in its grievance fueled, ideals driven revolutionary agenda. The upstarts took the NL and AA magnates by surprise, organizing a rival league under their noses in their own cities, pillaging a majority of their star players, completing the season without any member clubs dropping out, and outselling the established leagues at the gate. Logically, the PL ought to have persevered into 1891 and beyond, either absorbing or making peace with the NL and AA, and creating a template for management/labor relations outside of the mainstream of 19th century practice. PL owners, however, in a panic at their deficits, quickly agreed to consolidation and buyout offers from their slyer and more seasoned competitors, and abandoned their Brotherhood partners. So instead of inheriting the professional baseball world with a player/management relationship eighty years ahead of its time, the PL folded.

The renegade players were compelled to return to their former masters under working conditions of the *status quo ante*, the Brotherhood was broken, and the AA was effectively eviscerated as a viable competitor for the NL. The National League would monopolize its hold on big league baseball until the turn of the century when, through hubris and short-sighted mismanagement, the American League was born.

George Davis is our newest future Hall of Famer on the leaders' board.

THREE STARS WITH UNIQUE NICKNAMES WHO LED THEIR TEAMS TO PENNANTS IN 1890

Abram 'Hardy' Richardson led the heavy hitting Players League with 16 HRs and 152 RBIs, the second highest total in Big League Baseball's short history, to earn the Boston Reds the sole Players League pennant.

William 'Chicken' Wolf led the AA in hitting and in hits to help Louisville to its first and only pennant. Chicken went on to hit .360 in the World's Series and led all players with 8 RBI.

Thomas 'Oyster' Burns led the NL with 13 HRs and 128 RBIs in boosting Brooklyn to its second consecutive pennant.

1891

1891 proved to be the last season of operation for the American Association as an independent league. Significant steps had been taken by the AA to revitalize itself following the dissolution of the Players League after the 1890 season. However, the AA's long record of mismanagement in combination with many years of being undermined by the National League, their partner in the National Agreement, finally took its toll.

During the course of its decade long period of operation the AA had repeatedly lost franchises to the NL in major cities. Although nothing in the National Agreement, the peace treaty between the two leagues in effect since 1883, forbade the movement of a team from one league to another, the AA never protested strongly enough to discourage the NL from accepting deserters. The roster of major population centers lost from the AA to the NL, Pittsburgh, Cleveland, Cincinnati, and Brooklyn, together with the badly managed dissolution of the New York Metropolitans in 1887, which also showed traces of NL fingerprints, left the AA at a competitive disadvantage with the NL for a fan base. After losing a dispute over whether former AA star Harry Stovey could move to the NL after the collapse of the Players League following the 1890 season, the AA decided it had had enough of the NL as a working partner and withdrew from the National Agreement. Had this action been taken some years earlier, when AA prospects were brighter, it may have forced the NL to make concessions. However, coming when it did, the abrogation of the National Agreement simply encouraged the NL to woo other AA stars into the NL fold.

The AA had sought to strengthen itself for 1891 by dropping the teams from Toledo, Rochester, and Syracuse and looking to teams from the dissolved Players League to bolster the AA ranks. The AA co-opted the strong PL pennant winner from Boston while the PL Philadelphia club replaced the AA's insolvent Philadelphia club. Washington and a new Cincinnati club were also added to keep the AA roster of teams at eight. The Cincinnati team folded in August and was replaced by Milwaukee.

The eight team NL moved intact from 1890 into 1891. The League enjoyed the influx of its former players from the PL as well as a number of former AA stars once the AA pulled out of the National Agreement. Both leagues played about 140 games in 1891.

On the field it was an all Boston championship in both leagues.

In the AA the Boston Reds repeated their pennant winning performance from the PL the previous season, finishing eight and one half games ahead of von der Ahe's Browns. Big Dan Brouthers, Hugh Duffy, Duke Farrell, and Tom Brown paced the offense, with Brown leading the league in hits, runs, triples, and steals. George Haddock and veteran Charlie Buffinton combined to go 63-20 from the pitcher's box.

In the NL yet another controversy engulfed Cap Anson's Chicago club. Ahead of second place Boston in mid-September by six and one half games, Chicago went into a tailspin while Boston got hot, winning eighteen and losing one with one tie. During its winning streak Boston played five consecutive games against New York in which a number of New York's regulars, including Roger Connor, either did not play or made token appearances. Chicago management howled that New York deliberately held out its regulars to keep the Chicagoans from winning the pennant. Whether any such conspiracy, in fact, occurred was never proven, but Chicago certainly did not help itself by playing sub - .500 ball from mid-September and losing its last four games.

Regardless of the existence, or not, of any foul play against Chicago, the pennant belonged to Boston and second year manager Frank Selee by three and one half games. The Beaneaters powerful offense was led by shortstop Herman Long, first baseman Tommy Tucker, third sacker Billy Nash, and erstwhile AA star Harry Stovey, who led the NL in triples and tied for the lead in homers with sixteen. Boston also featured a great pitching staff composed of John Clarkson, Kid Nichols, and Harry Staley. One of the trio pitched in every game during Boston's pennant drive beginning in mid-September.

An all – Boston World's Championship Series was thwarted when the NL, sensing it had the AA on the ropes, refused the AA challenge, lamely citing the absence of the National Agreement. Consequently, no post-season championship series occurred for the first time since 1884.

Here are the leaders on offense, defense, and pitching for each league. Relief pitching continues to be an afterthought in strategy. In any event no pitching splits are available.

NATIONAL LEAGUE

	OFFENSE		DEFENSE
C	Jack Clements – 209 – Philadelphia	C	**Chief Zimmer – 5 – Cleveland**
1B	Roger Connor – 295 – New York	1B	Cap Anson – 4 – Chicago
2B	Cupid Childs – 309 – Cleveland	2B	Bid McPhee – 4 – Cincinnati
SS	Herman Long – 301 – Boston	SS	Herman Long – 2 – Boston
3B	Arlie Latham – 279 – Cincinnati	3B	None
LF	**Billy Hamilton – 344 – Philadelphia**	LF	Billy Hamilton – 2 – Philadelphia
RF	Sam Thompson – 291 – Philadelphia	RF	Sam Thompson – 4 – Philadelphia
CF	George Davis – 307 – Cleveland	**CF**	**Mike Griffin – 5 – Brooklyn**
P	Kid Gleason/John Clarkson – 92 - Philadelphia/Boston	P	Kid Nichols/Scott Stratton – 2 – Boston/Pitt(NL)-Lou(AA)
Multi	Harry Stovey – 298 – Boston		

Boston scored the most runs in the NL, yielded the fewest, and boasted the widest run differential by a considerable margin. Lefty batter Billy Hamilton was a run scoring machine for Philadelphia. The fleet footed left fielder led the league in hits (179), walks (102), steals (111), and runs scored (141) on his way to claiming best hitter laurels.

Best Pitcher: Bill Hutchison - .681 – Chicago

Best Reliever: TBD

Hutchison basically tried to do it all by himself from the pitcher's box for Chicago in 1891. The righthander led the league in innings pitched, games pitched, and wins with forty four. Hutchison threw nearly half of Chicago's innings in '91, a considerable achievement in a 137 game schedule. In Hutchison's decisions Chicago compiled a record of 44 – 19. In other games they were only 38 – 34. In the final reckoning Anson's crew needed more quality arms to compete with Boston's stellar hurlers.

AMERICAN ASSOCIATION

	OFFENSE		DEFENSE
C	Deacon McGuire – 196 – Washington	C	Morgan Murphy – 2 – Boston
1B	Big Dan Brouthers – 346 – Boston	1B	Mike LeHane – 3 – Columbus
2B	Bill Hallman – 262 – Philadelphia	2B	Cub Stricker – 4 – Boston
SS	Paul Radford – 263 – Boston	SS	Tom Corcoran/Bob Wheelock – 2 – Philadelphia/Columbus
3B	Denny Lyons – 284 – St. Louis	3B	Pete Gilbert – 2 – Baltimore
LF	Tip O'Neill – 293 – St. Louis	LF	George Wood – 3 – Philadelphia
RF	Hugh Duffy – 358 – Boston	RF	Chicken Wolf – 3 – Louisville
CF	**Tom Brown – 376 – Boston**	**CF**	**Farmer Weaver – 6 – Louisville**
P	Jack Stivetts – 148 – St. Louis	P	Scott Stratton – 3 – Pitt(NL)-Lou(AA)
Multi	George Van Haltren – 328 – Baltimore		

Boston and St. Louis blew away the rest of the league in both offense and defense in 1891. The two clubs far outscored their opponents and, as the list of offensive leaders illustrates, the Reds and Browns dominated most offensive positions. More telling was the run differential tabulated by both teams, over three hundred more runs scored than yielded for Boston, and over two hundred for St. Louis. The next closest team claimed a run differential of only fifty two.

Best Pitcher: Sadie McMahon - .586 – Baltimore

Best Reliever: TBD

Like Hutchison in the NL, McMahon led his loop in innings pitched, games started, and wins, with thirty five. Also, like Hutchison, McMahon threw nearly half his team's innings in a 139 game schedule. In McMahon's decisions the Orioles boasted a record of 35 – 24. In the rest of their games the tally was only 36 – 39. The righty achieved best pitcher for the second consecutive season.

In 1890 and 1891 the NL was able to dispose of two formidable competing organizations, the Players League and the American Association. Additionally, NL management had broken the back of the players' Brotherhood and, without any competing major league, would enjoy maximum bargaining power with its players in a shrinking players market.

It should be noted that the AA, in its final season, did complete the schedule and anoint a pennant winner, the powerful Boston Reds, a prodigious offensive team which won pennants in back to back seasons in different leagues. That the Reds were never given the opportunity to establish a record in post-season play is one of the more regrettable consequences of the nineteenth century baseball dynamic.

The formal breakup of the AA occurred after the conclusion of the season. The owner of the Boston Reds, seeking to divest himself of his baseball interests, could not find a buyer for his team in the AA. Then, in the absence of the protection of a National Agreement, most of the regulars from von der Ahe's strong St. Louis team defected to the NL. Having lost all his bargaining chips, the Browns mercurial owner was compelled to cave in to amalgamation of the AA with the NL. The ten year existence of the AA as an independent organization was finished.

The legacy of the AA into the modern day is significant. The AA introduced Sunday baseball where permitted by law, legitimized the sale of beer and alcohol at games, evolved the concept of impartial umpire teams, and provided the genesis of the present day Pirates, Dodgers, Cardinals, and Reds. The business competition fostered by the formation of the AA increased employment opportunities for players on the big league level, generated a boost in player salaries, at least for a while, provided thousands upon thousands of additional fans with the entertainment of big league baseball, and established the foundation of the modern World Series. Not incidentally, NL pennant winners defeated AA pennant winners outright only four times in seven tries in the World's Championship Series.

Kid Nichols is our newest future Hall of Famer on the leaders' board.

Harry Stovey was a vital cog on championship teams in three leagues during a career spanning 1880 to 1893. A unique combination of power and speed, Stovey led his league in HRs, triples, or steals a total of 11 times. Winning pennants with Philadelphia of the AA in 1883, Boston of the NL in 1891, and the Boston Reds of the PL in 1890, the firstbaseman/outfielder has somehow been overlooked for the Hall of Fame. Stovey's insistence on joining the NL after 1890 hastened the demise of the AA as an independent league.

Centerfielder Tom Brown was the AA's best hitter in its final independent season, leading the league in hits (189), triples (21), steals (106), and runs scored (177) for pennant winning Boston.

1892

Amalgamation between the National League and American Association following the 1891 season resulted in the formation of a twelve team league for 1892. The amalgamated league included all the NL teams from 1891 plus St. Louis, Baltimore, Louisville, and Washington from the former AA. An ambitious season schedule of 154 games was set which represented the most regular season games ever.

Although the consolidation marked a cessation of hostility between the former rival leagues, the AA clubs absorbed into the amalgamated league found themselves to be at a considerable competitive disadvantage. Player defections from the AA clubs in the wake of the abrogation of the National Agreement in 1891 had reduced the four AA survivors to second division also-rans for 1892. Not only did the former AA clubs occupy the final four slots in the overall 1892 standings, but St. Louis, once the premiere franchise in the AA with four consecutive pennants from 1885 through 1888, finished a dismal eleventh overall. Baltimore, another AA survivor, ushered in the record 154 game schedule with 101 losses in last place, overall.

Despite the NL having won a baseball monopoly through the failure of its competitors, management had come to recognize the financial value and fan interest in a World's Championship Series. Without a rival league to furnish a World's Series opponent, and fearing that the expanded schedule of games could adversely impact fan interest in the regular season, the League established a split season for 1892. The first half of the season would result in a champion which would then play the champion of the second half of the season in a World's Championship Series.

Defending NL champion Boston narrowly finished ahead of Brooklyn to win the 'first half' pennant. The Beaneaters boosted their powerful 1891 lineup featuring Herman Long, Billy Nash, and Tommy Tucker with future Hall of Famers Hugh Duffy and Tommy McCarthy from the AA ranks. Also from the AA came former St. Louis ace Jack Stivetts, bolstering an already formidable pitching staff consisting of Kid Nichols, Harry Staley, and John Clarkson. In a cost saving measure emblematic of management's superior bargaining position over the players, the champs released longtime pitching star Clarkson on June 30 as a consequence of a salary dispute. Cleveland, buried eleven games behind Boston on June 30, promptly signed the veteran to add experience to their fledgling staff for the second half.

The acquisition of Clarkson contributed to a resurgent second half for Cleveland. The ex-Beaneater compiled a record of 17 – 10 for the Spiders in twenty-nine appearances propelling them ahead of Boston for the 'second half' pennant. Cleveland's revamped pitching staff, consisting of Clarkson and the youthful duo of Cy Young and Nig Cuppy, figured in nearly every decision for the Spiders in the second half, combining to go 51 – 19. The Spiders also featured a balanced offense spearheaded by second baseman Cupid Childs, future Hall of Fame left fielder Jesse Burkett, and first sacker Jake Virtue.

It would be defending NL champ Boston versus Cleveland in the first 'split season' World's Championship Series.

A best of nine championship series commenced in Cleveland with one of the most brilliant pitching duels in post-season history. Six thousand fans witnessed Cy Young and Jack Stivetts match zeroes for eight innings. In the Cleveland ninth, Jesse Burkett bunted for a hit. George Davis singled, putting two men on base with only one out. Ed McKean then blistered a grounder, but directly at shortstop Herman Long, who tossed to second for the force on Davis. While second baseman Joe Quinn argued with the umpire concerning claimed interference by Davis with a possible double play, Burkett, now at third, took his chance and headed home. Quinn was alert to the gamble and fired home to King Kelly who applied the tag with less than a foot separating the Spiders from an opening game ninth inning lead. With the best scoring chance of the game for either team eradicated the game continued into extra innings until it was ended after the bottom of the eleventh due to darkness in a scoreless tie. Young and Stivetts scattered ten singles between them in an unusually crisply played game.

The tie turned out to be the best outing of the series for the Spiders as they lost the next five in a row to Boston and manager Frank Selee, who claimed his second straight pennant and first World's Championship. Hugh Duffy was the hitting star for Boston in the Series with twelve hits, nine RBIs, and a .462 batting average.

Here is the best starting pitcher for 1892 together with the leaders on offense and defense. No significant relief pitching is occurring.

	OFFENSE		DEFENSE
C	Chief Zimmer – 200 – Cleveland	C	Jack Clements – 2 – Philadelphia
1B	**Big Dan Brouthers – 368 – Brooklyn**	1B	Jake Beckley/Charlie Comiskey – 3 – Pittsburgh/Cincinnati
2B	Cupid Childs – 305 – Cleveland	2B	Lou Bierbauer – 4 – Pittsburgh
SS	Herman Long – 292 – Boston	SS	Hughie Jennings/Bob Allen – 3 – Louisville/Philadelphia
3B	Billy Nash – 268 – Boston	3B	Billy Shindle – 3 – Baltimore
LF	Billy Hamilton – 302 – Philadelphia	LF	Billy Hamilton – 3 – Philadelphia
RF	Sam Thompson – 312 – Philadelphia	RF	None
CF	Hugh Duffy – 312 – Boston	CF	Jimmy McAleer/Mike Griffin – 3 – Cleveland/Brooklyn
P	Jack Stivetts – 128 – Boston	P	Kid Gleason – 2 – St. Louis
Multi	Bug Holliday – 294 – Cincinnati		

Boston and Cleveland boasted the best run differential in the league in the combined standings. While the Spiders were tops during the regular season in that category, Boston emphatically proved their offensive superiority in the championship series, 31 – 15.

Best Starting Pitcher: Bill Hutchison - .668 – Chicago

Best Relief Pitcher: TBD

Hutchison ruled the roost for the second consecutive season, leading the league in strikeouts, innings pitched, games pitched, and tied in wins with thirty six. The diminutive righthander also achieved the best strikeouts to walks/hbp ratio for full-time starters.

So that's it for 1892, the first year of amalgamation. Notwithstanding the pathetic performance of the gutted clubs from the AA, no teams dropped out of the league, the 'split season' scheme resulted in a successful post-season championship series, and no internecine bickering occurred between rival leagues. On the minus side, attendance was down and many players felt aggrieved with salary restrictions and a reserve clause which limited their bargaining power.

Jake Beckley and Hughie Jennings are the newest future Hall of Famers on the leaders' board, bringing the total to twenty four. Here they are; Harry Wright, Al Spalding, Cap Anson, George Wright, Deacon White, Orator O'Rourke, John M. Ward, King Kelly, Roger Connor, Pud Galvin, Big Dan Brouthers, Ned Hanlon, Charlie Comiskey, Bid McPhee, Tim Keefe, Old Hoss Radbourn, John Clarkson, Sam Thompson, Buck Ewing, Tommy McCarthy, George Davis, Kid Nichols, Hughie Jennings, and Jake Beckley. While some of the aforementioned actually earned Hall of Fame laurels based on their careers as managers or executives, their presence on the leaders' board demonstrates that they possessed superior skills on the diamond before hanging up their spikes.

Hutchison led the NL three years running in games (71, 66, 75), innings (603, 561, 622), and wins (41, 44, 36). The righty achieved best pitcher for 1891 and 1892 but the toil on his throwing arm ruined his effectiveness for the remainder of his career.

Hugh Duffy joined Boston from the AA for 1892 and led the team in runs, hits, triples, and batting average. In the split season World's Series in 1892 he bedeviled the Spiders, leading all batters with 9 RBIs and a .462 batting average.

Brouthers, playing for Brooklyn in 1892, had an incredible season, scoring 121 runs, driving in 124, and leading the league in hits and batting average on his way to achieving best hitter by a comfortable margin.

1893

The amalgamated twelve team league returned intact for 1893.

The league scrapped the 'split season' format for 1893 which pitted the 'first half' winner against the 'second half' winner in a post-season championship series at the end of the season. The glaring flaw in this formulation was that the 'first half' winner and 'second half' winner could end up being the same team. This created a scenario where the 'first half' winner might deliberately let up or even throw games during the second half to ensure a post-season opponent. No alternative post-season plan was established for 1893.

Management also implemented a number of measures to address diminished attendance the previous season. The schedule was reduced from 154 games to 136 games. A more significant change, however, resonates to the present day. Concerned that lack of offense was adversely impacting attendance, the league voted to increase the pitching distance by five feet, from fifty five and one half feet to sixty and one half feet. That's right, sixty feet six inches.

In effect, the pitching box was eliminated. Before pitching the ball the hurler was now required to keep one foot in contact with a twelve inch wide boundary plate, or 'rubber', instead of the back line of the, now, non-existent pitching box. From this position he could take one additional step towards the batter prior to delivering the ball. While the concept of elevating the pitcher with a 'mound' was only beginning to gain traction, the pitching distance of sixty feet six inches has remained constant from 1893 to the present day.

The historical road to the sixty feet six inch pitching distance was a tortuous one. Organized league play commenced in 1871. In that season the pitching distance between home plate and the release point of the ball was forty five feet. Pitchers were required to throw underhand but could engage in all manner of gyrations, including a running start, from within a six foot by six foot pitching box before delivering the pitch. No base was awarded to a hit batsman. Batters were entitled to call for high or low pitches. As many as eight or nine bad ones had to go by before a base on balls would be declared. Although three strikes were required for a strikeout, non-swinging strikes were inconsistently called.

Twenty two seasons were played before big league baseball settled on the pitching distance, style of pitching, and ball/strike calculations one would consider recognizable today. Still to come, however, was the counting of foul balls as strikes.

During those twenty two seasons underhand pitching gave way, first, to sidearm, and then, to over the shoulder deliveries allowing for a greater diversity of pitches.

The dimensions of the pitching box began to fluctuate in 1879 as the increased diversity of pitches put the batter at a disadvantage. By 1881 the batter was at such a severe disadvantage that the pitching distance was increased five feet, to fifty feet. Continuing concern over lack of offense prompted both the NL and AA in 1887 to eliminate the pitcher's multiple step delivery and anchor his back foot to a pitching line at the back of the pitcher's box fifty five feet six inches away from home plate.

All the while hitters slowly benefitted from reductions in the number of errant pitches required for a walk and, in that same year of 1887, actually getting a fourth strike before striking out. Reversion to the three strikes yer' out rule the following season again stifled offenses.

The four ball walk rule instituted for 1889 rescued sinking batting averages, but only temporarily, as both NL and AA batting averages took significant dips over the next two seasons. Another precipitous decline in batting average, together with disappointing attendance totals, finally prompted the NL to extend the pitching distance the final five feet in 1893.

The common thread in this evolution from forty five feet to sixty feet six inches was the goal of reducing the pitcher's advantage over the hitter, to wit, more offense.

1893 resulted in an orgy of offense with the institution of the sixty foot, six inch pitching distance.

In order to appreciate the effect of the new pitching dimensions on offensive production, consider the following chart:

	1892	**1893**
Approximate games per team	155	131
Home Runs	417	460
Triples	1,010	1,047
Doubles	2,007	2,197
Singles	12,209	12,209
League Batting Average	.245	.280
League Earned Run Average	3.28	4.66

Even though there were fewer games in 1893, there were more total hits, more extra base hits in every category, and, remarkably, the exact same number of singles, but in 136 fewer games. Pitchers yielded over an additional run per game, and batting averages skyrocketed.

Examining the impact from a different perspective, in 1892, from the old pitching distance, seventeen pitchers who threw at least two hundred innings struck out more batters than they walked, including future Hall of Famers Cy Young, Amos Rusie, Kid Nichols, John Clarkson, and Tim Keefe. In 1893, from the extended pitching distance, no pitchers who threw over two hundred innings struck out more batters than they walked. The above mentioned Hall of Famers all walked more batters than they struck out in 1893.

There were certainly jumps in offense and ERA in previous seasons when the pitching distance was lengthened, from 1886 to 1887, for example. But the effect in 1893 was so significant that it reverberates into the modern era. Consider that in 1993 the batting average in major league baseball stood at .265, compared to .280 in 1893. Major league ERA in 1993 was 4.18. Major league ERA in 1893 stood at 4.66. Finally, offenses averaged 12 hits per game in 1993 compared to 20 hits per game in 1893. One can't help but be reminded of the Bugs Bunny cartoon where the Gashouse Gorillas form a conga line around the bases against the hapless pitcher for the Teetotalers while scoring runs in the dozens.

On the field Boston coasted to its third consecutive pennant under manager Frank Selee. The offense was propelled by a solid lineup featuring future Hall of Famers Hugh Duffy and

Tommy McCarthy, as well as Billy Nash, Herman Long, Bobby Lowe, and Tommy Tucker, who all enjoyed outstanding seasons. On the distant boundary plate Kid Nichols, Jack Stivetts, and Harry Staley each contributed in excess of 260 innings pitched, with Nichols throwing 425. Pittsburgh, eleven and one half games off Boston's pace in mid-September, finished in second place by five games.

Here are the leaders on offense, defense, and starting pitcher for 1893. Relief pitching continues to be an afterthought despite the added burden put on pitching staffs by the increased pitching distance.

	OFFENSE		DEFENSE
C	John Grim – 189 – Louisville	C	John Grim – 2 – Louisville
1B	Jake Beckley – 313 – Pittsburgh	1B	Jake Beckley – 4 – Pittsburgh
2B	Cupid Childs – 326 – Cleveland	2B	Bid McPhee – 5 – Cincinnati
SS	Ed McKean – 338 – Cleveland	SS	Germany Smith – 4 – Cincinnati
3B	George Davis – 341 – New York	3B	Billy Nash – 2 – Boston
LF	**Ed Delahanty – 399 – Philadelphia**	**LF**	**Ed Delahanty – 6 – Philadelphia**
RF	Sam Thompson – 366 – Philadelphia	RF	Patsy Donovan – 3 – Pittsburgh
CF	Hugh Duffy – 378 – Boston	CF	Tom Brown – 4 – Louisville
P	Frank Killen – 104 – Pittsburgh	P	Frank Dwyer/Scott Stratton – 2 – Cincinnati/Louisville
Multi	Tommy McCarthy – 326 - Boston		

While Boston did not place many players among the leaders on offense or defense, the Beaneaters still managed to enjoy the widest run differential in the league.

Best Starting Pitcher: Cy Young - .444 – Cleveland

Best Relief Pitcher: TBD

Young and Amos Rusie were the best pitchers of 1893, with Young edging Rusie by a slim margin for best pitcher honors. In a year when pitchers were severely tested, Young tied for third in strikeouts, walking only one more than he struck out, a considerable accomplishment that season. He was also the ace on the third place Spiders' staff with 33 wins against 16 losses. In games where Young did not get a decision, Cleveland was 40 – 39.

So that's the story for 1893, when hitters held sway. Bid McPhee of Cincinnati achieved best fielder at second base for a remarkable eleventh time. Big Ed Delahanty and Cy Young are our newest future Hall of Famers on the leaders board, bringing the total to twenty six.

In a season when hitting held sway, Delahanty of Philadelphia was the best hitter. With 19 HRs and 146 RBIs, 'Big Ed' narrowly missed a triple crown, batting .368. Skilled afield as well as at bat, he was also the best leftfielder of 1893. Selected for the Hall of Fame 1945.

In a season when pitchers were severely tested, 26 year old Cy Young rose to the challenge. Winning 33 games for Cleveland, the durable righty walked only one more than he struck out on his way to achieving his first of many best pitcher honors. Elected to the Hall of Fame 1937.

Epilogue to Volume 1

Big League Baseball's arrival in 1871 was an inevitable consequence of the burgeoning professionalism of the mid to late 1860's.

Local rivalries during that time begat competition to attract top performers who would only play for pay. Regional rivalries created the impetus for league play, bragging rights, and the unavoidable presence of the bean counters and the bottom line.

The struggles experienced by the National Association during its five year existence highlighted the need for a business model utilizing a stronger central authority. Indeed, in its first years of operation, the National League, through its authoritarian and opinionated president, William Hulbert, banned teams for failing to complete schedules and banned players for conspiring with gamblers to throw ballgames.

Hulbert, however, was a deeply flawed leader whose original motivations in promulgating the creation of the National League were mixed. On the one hand he wanted the League to be run by business minded moguls with an eye on the bottom line. On the other hand, however, he focused on his own bottom line as majority shareholder of the Chicago club in the NA and, later, the NL. Consequently, growth of the NL was stunted by Hulbert's antipathy towards the eastern cities and his resultant inability to look beyond the success of his own club as being in the best interests of the League as a whole.

As a consequence of Hulbert's shortsightedness new teams were not established in the country's strongest markets in New York and Philadelphia. While Hulbert's Chicago club gobbled up pennants, other cities dropped out of the League at an alarming rate reminiscent of the NA years and the NL's slate of scheduled games lagged behind those in the latter seasons of the NA.

In 1882, six years after the founding of the NL, fans and organizers starved for big league baseball by restrictive NL admission policies spawned the competing American Association. The AA allowed baseball to prosper. More cities and more fans could now experience and enjoy Big League Baseball. More players could find big league jobs at big league salaries. More ancillary businesses could feed off the growth of the sport. New

York and Philadelphia re-joined the Big League ranks of cities in the competing leagues, Big League entertainment was made available on Sundays, where permitted by law, and in some parks one could buy a beer, further enhancing the experience of attending a game, while, at the same time, bolstering management's profit margin.

With a competing league the concept of an overall or 'World's Champion' was born, providing yet another basis for fan interest, owner profit, and player pay. While the earliest efforts at post-season play were clumsily orchestrated, by 1889 16,000 fans showed up for game two of the World's Championship Series in Brooklyn against rival New York.

Throughout the 1880's, however, pernicious undercurrents of avarice and hostility undercut progress.

Although Hulbert was dead, his characteristic shortsightedness lived on through the repeated efforts of NL management to hamstring their business partners in the AA, as well as to weaken and ultimately cause the dissolution of successful teams in New York and Detroit. Management in both leagues imposed onerous salary restrictions on their players through the imposition of a reserve clause in player contracts which severely limited players' bargaining powers, and by repeatedly threatening to impose salary caps, among other abuses. Finally, management and players alike collaborated to exclude players of color from playing on the Big League level.

Labor unrest caused the first great breach in the sport with the formation by unionized, dissatisfied players of a rival league, the Players League, in 1890. The PL, filled with stars from both leagues, incorporated a number of player friendly salary reforms in cooperation with new management interests and actually outdrew the NL and AA at the gate. Clever maneuvering by more seasoned NL owners, however, separated the renegade players from their fledgling owners, causing the PL to dissolve after its first season.

With the players subdued the NL next set its avaricious sights on the weakened AA. Once again, slyer NL owners carried the day, raiding AA rosters when AA management foolishly abrogated the peace treaty in effect between the two leagues since 1883. With their best bargaining chips gone, the few remaining AA clubs settled for amalgamation with the NL in 1892.

The NL, now swelled with success after vanquished its business competitors, took a hard line with the players, who now had nowhere else to play. Schedules were increased and a 'split season' was established to arrange for an intra-league World's Championship series.

The final arbiters of these sanguine policies, however, were the fans, who stayed away. Disappointing attendance in 1892 caused management to reduce schedules, slash salaries even further, dispense with the 'split season' format, eliminate any post-season championship, and, in the hope that greater offense would improve attendance, impose the sixty feet six inches pitching distance which has endured to the present day.

1893 witnessed improvements both at the gate and in the financial ledgers for Big League Baseball. After twenty two seasons management had succeeded in bringing profitability to its franchises, harnessing the behavior and ambitions of its players, presenting an exciting spectacle of sport to fans in twelve cities from Boston to St. Louis, and establishing itself as the most successful spectator team sport in American history.

What could go wrong?

Appendix A
Tabulating Offense

For all full-time offensive players the same tabulation formula is used. It looks like this:

R-HR + 1B/4 + 2B/2 + 3B x .75 + RBI-HR + HR + W-K/4 + HBP/4 + SB-CS/3 + BAVG x 100 =

R-HR, RBI-HR: I fully appreciate that runs scored as well as runs batted in are products of what one's teammates are doing. In the case of a run scored, you get on base, someone else drives you in. In the case of a RBI, someone else gets on base, you drive him in. The fact remains, however, that runs scored are the basis of how baseball games are won or lost and that players proficient at scoring them or driving them in should be credited for their accomplishment. So I compromised by including runs scored and RBIs in the formula together with all the other things the batter does independently of his teammates. The removal of HRs from the runs and RBIs computation puts sluggers and speedsters on the same footing in those categories.

1B/4, 2B/2, 3B x .75, HR: These are weighted in much the same manner as slugging average. In other words, a single is one quarter of a run, a double is one half of a run, etc.

W-K/4: A walk is not quite as good as a hit, notwithstanding Little League chants to the contrary. Players are credited for their walks only to the degree they exceed strikeouts, so players are penalized for strikeouts, which are useless in generating anything on the field which may produce a run. However, a batter will never receive a negative value for strikeouts. A player whose strikeouts exceed walks will receive a zero value in that category.

HBP/4: Getting hit by a pitch is nearly identical to a walk, except that it hurts, more often than not. Consequently, HBPs get their own, unmitigated, category.

SB-CS/3: Steals are credited only to the extent that they exceed 'caught stealings'. Furthermore, a runner whose 'caught stealings' exceed his steals WILL receive a negative value. The runner is penalized for removing himself from having any possibility of scoring a run after successfully getting on base.

BAVG x 100: I agonized over whether batting average ought to be included in the formula. This is because batting average, by itself, has nothing to do with accumulating bases or scoring runs. Ultimately, I decided that players with good batting averages were more proficient at getting on base and should receive credit for it. Additionally, batting average was not covered by any other part of the formula.

So that's the formula. What I especially love about the tabulation is that it is simple, easy to understand, and can be applied by anybody, unlike some other statistical measures like WAR or WAA. Essentially, a 5th or

6th grader can apply the formula if a player's stats are available. The formula lucidly demonstrates a hitter's strengths and weakness relative to his peers.

It's more fun to illustrate.

Let's take two leftfielders from the same era in their MVP seasons, Pete Rose in 1973 and Carl Yastrzemski in 1967. Both were full-time players in leftfield in those seasons. Stats are from Retrosheet.org.

$$R-HR + 1B/4 + 2B/2 + 3B \times .75 + RBI-HR + HR + W-K/4 + HBP/4 + SB-CS/3 + BAVG \times 100 = X$$

Pete Rose 1973

100 + 45 + 18 + 6 + 59 + 5 + 6 + 2 + 1 + 34 = 276

Carl Yastrzemski 1967

68 + 28 + 16 + 3 + 77 + 44 + 6 + 1 + 1 + 33 = 277

Well looky that, the slugger and the on base guy are just about dead even

For the purposes of this book only full-time players are tabulated. So who is a full-time player? A full-time player is one who played in at least 75% of his team's innings played. Innings played is more accurate than games played since a player who appears in a game may not play the entire game. Happily, innings played are available on sites such as *retrosheet.org* and *baseball-reference.com*.

For example, in 1871 Harry Wright played 248.33 innings in centerfield for Boston. All players who played centerfield for Boston played 276 innings. Harry Wright played 90% of those innings, hence, he was a full-time player at that position since he meets the 75% threshold. Some players log innings at multiple positions, such as Ross Barnes in 1871 for Boston. He played both 2B and SS. Using the same method of counting innings played, Barnes played 51% of his team's innings at 2B and 48% of Boston's innings at SS for a total of 99% of innings played, easily putting him over the 75% threshold. Barnes would be considered a multiple position player for 1871. He would not be compared with other shortstops or second basemen for that season, only other multiple position players.

By comparison, Frank Barrows played a total of 150 innings at various positions for Boston that season. His total innings played only comes to 54% of Boston's total innings, hence, Frank would not be considered a full-time player at any individual position or a multi position player and would not be tabulated for that season.

Players who spend time with multiple teams in a season can still be tabulated if they meet the 75% threshold for their combined innings played for both teams. In this circumstance innings played are considered with the average of the innings both teams played. Easier to illustrate by example. In 1979 Ted Sizemore played for the Cubs and Red Sox. He combined for 1,008.67 innings for both. Boston and Chicago combined for 2,878 innings played, averaging to 1,439 each. Sizemore played for 70% of the average innings combined, or 1,008.67/1,439. 70% is short of the 75% threshold, hence, he would not be considered a full-time player for either team for 1979.

The exception to the 75% threshold is for catchers. My research disclosed that the position of catcher was, by far, the most difficult for players to log the requisite number of innings. Consequently, the threshold for catchers is 66% of their team's innings played. A DH is given credit for 9 innings played if he plays a complete game at DH.

Finally, these offensive scores are comparative in nature. Shortstops are compared to shortstops, not first basemen. Centerfielders are compared to centerfielders, not rightfielders. Consequently, each season will feature a best offensive performer for each position. I would also caution against comparing offensive scores for players from different eras. There are too many variables from era to era which impact offensive output, such as number of games played, number of baseballs available for use, whether spitballs are legal, etc. In sum, although tempting, Ichiro's offensive score should not be compared to Wee Willie Keeler's. Of course, no one is stopping you from doing that for fun. You have the formula.

Appendix B
Best Hitter by Season

1871 – Ross Barnes

1872 – Ross Barnes

1873 – Ross Barnes

1874 – Cal McVey

1875 – Ross Barnes

1876 – Ross Barnes

1877 – Deacon White

1878 – Cap Anson

1879 – Paul Hines

1880 – Abner Dalrymple

1881 – Cap Anson

1882 – Cap Anson NL   Ed Swartwood AA

1883 – Dan Brouthers NL   John Reilly AA

1884 – King Kelly NL   Harry Stovey AA

1885 – Cap Anson NL   Henry Larkin AA

1886 – Cap Anson NL   Henry Larkin AA

1887 – Sam Thompson NL   Tip O'Neill AA

1888 – Dan Brouthers NL   John Reilly AA

1889 – Roger Connor NL   Harry Stovey AA

1890 – Hub Collins NL   Spud Johnson AA   Hugh Duffy PL

1891 – Billy Hamilton NL   Tom Brown AA

1892 – Dan Brouthers

1893 – Ed Delahanty

5 – Ross Barnes, Cap Anson   3 – Dan Brouthers   2 – John Reilly, Harry Stovey, Henry Larkin

Appendix C
Rating Pitchers - Starters

There are two different formulas for rating pitchers. One applies to starting appearances, the other to relief appearances.

Let's begin with starters. The formula looks like this:

Wins Above Team/Team Wins + Starter's Ks − (W+HBP)/Starter's Innings Pitched + Starter IP/Team IP − His Relief IP − Starter's HR Allowed/Starter's IP =

It looks complicated, but, in fact, it's only four factors and really quite simple.

Wins Above Team/Team Wins: Some purists take the position, like the consideration of runs scored and RBIs for hitters, that a pitcher's won/lost record is the product of what his team does for him, both offensively and defensively. By this reasoning, pitchers on good teams will always have an advantage in accumulating wins over pitchers on poorer teams. This logic is unassailable. However, the game of baseball is premised on wins and losses and, for better or worse, pitchers have been awarded decisions from the earliest days of keeping score, consequently, I consider it heretical to ignore won/lost records for starting pitchers. So, I compromised. Won/lost records for starting pitchers are incorporated into the formula but only as a percentage of wins above team divided by total team wins. This way, the pitcher is given credit for his won/lost record but only relative to the strength of his team. The way it works out, pitchers with good records on strong teams invariably end up with a lower number than pitchers with good records on poorer teams.

Let's illustrate with two such pitchers.

In 1970 Jim Palmer went 20 – 10 for the Orioles, who won 108 and lost 54 on their way to winning the World Series. First, we calculate Palmer's 'wins above team'. Palmer's winning percentage is .667. Without Palmer, the record of the Orioles is 88 – 44, also .667. Palmer's winning percentage, .667, minus the Orioles' winning percentage without him, in this case, also .667, equals 0. Multiplying Palmer's total decisions times 0 gives you his 'wins above team', in this case, still 0. Palmer has 0 'wins above team'. Next, we divide Palmer's 'wins above team' by the Orioles' total wins. 0/108 equals 0. This would be Palmer's value in this category.

In 1943 Schoolboy Rowe went 14 – 8 as a starter for the Phillies, who were dreadful, going 64 – 90 on their way to oblivion. Rowe's winning percentage was .636. Without Schoolboy, the failing Phillies were 50 – 82, a percentage of .379. Schoolboy's winning percentage, .636, minus the Phils' winning percentage without him, .379, equals .257. Multiplying Schoolboy's total decisions times .257 gives you his 'wins above team'.

22 x .257 = 5.654. Schoolboy has 5.654 'wins above team', a pretty substantial number. Finally, we divide Schoolboy's 'wins above team' by the Phillies' total wins. 5.654/64 equals .088. This would be Schoolboy's value in this category.

So, in this case, a 14 game winner on a crappy team ends up with a significantly stronger value than a 20 game winner on a fabulous team. Compromise achieved. By the way, it is possible to earn a negative value for this stat.

Starter's Ks – (W+HBP)/Starter's IP: This is a pure pitcher stat. The pitcher requires no assistance from his fielders to record a strikeout. The fielders, similarly, have little impact on whether a batter reaches a base on balls. Some catchers are gifted at framing pitches, but there is no stat for this…yet. The pitcher is entirely responsible for hitting a batter with a pitched ball. Essentially, pitchers are penalized by crediting them with their strikeouts only to the degree the strikeouts exceed walks and hit batsmen. The net of strikeouts minus walks and hit batsmen is then divided by the pitcher's innings pitched as a starter. A pitcher may receive a negative value in this category if his walks and hit batsmen exceed strikeouts. Consequently, pitchers do well in this category who are adept at strikeouts and who have good control. Pedro Martinez would do very well. Nolan Ryan would not. Stats earned in relief are not counted here if there is a breakdown of starter and relief stats available.

Starter IP/Team IP – His Relief IPs: This is a workhorse stat. The pitcher's innings as a starter are divided by the team's total innings pitched. His relief innings are pulled out of the team total so he is not competing against himself, if a breakdown of relief innings is available.

Starter HRs Allowed/Starter IPs: No one helps a pitcher yield a home run. It's entirely his fault, so he is penalized for it. The exception, of course, is for inside-the-park home runs. Unfortunately, inside-the-park home runs are not separately tabulated for each pitcher, so I cannot subtract them. This is more of an issue for 19th century and deadball era homeruns which left the yard to a lesser extent than the present day. The home run total yielded in a starting capacity is then divided by the innings pitched in a starting capacity. This value can never be a positive number. The best a pitcher can aspire to here is a 0. Once again, stats earned in relief are not counted here if a breakdown of starter and relief stats are available.

So that's the formula for starting pitchers. Three of the four stats are pitcher specific, which is to say, they are unaffected or minimally affected by teammates. For most seasons prior to 1901 statistical breakdowns of starter innings versus relief innings have not been tabulated. For those years in which relief pitching cannot be accurately measured, the pitching numbers, of necessity, must be combined. Happily, not much relief pitching was occurring in the period prior to 1901.

Well, enough jibber jabber. It's always more fun to illustrate with examples. I previously made reference to Pedro Martinez and Nolan Ryan. Let's compare them in a couple of their best seasons.

WAT/TW + Starter K –(W+HBP)/Starter IP + Starter IP/Team IP – His RIP - Starter HR/Starter IP

Martinez 1997 Montreal Expos 78 - 84

.075 + .949 + .167 - .066 = 1.125

Ryan 1977 California Angels 74 - 88

.052 + .428 + .208 - .040 = .648

As expected, Ryan's lack of control significantly reduced his score and, in fact, accounted for Martinez throttling him in the final total. Ryan struck out 341 in '77 but walked 204. He hit 9 batters. All of this in 299 innings. Pedro struck out 305 while walking only 67. He hit 9 batters. All this in 241.33 innings. Both played for lousy teams. Ryan was the greater workhorse. Pedro served up a greater percentage of dingers. It's only a formula, but of the two, who would you rather have?

Anyway, once all pitchers have received their rating, select starters are also rated for offense and defense according to the formulas for offensive and defensive players, which are detailed in the remaining appendices. Not all starters get this treatment because not all starters are created equal. Nolan Ryan who threw 299 innings in 1977 is not considered to be in the same category of accomplishment as teammate Gary Ross, who threw 53.33.

When all the starter innings for the league are logged, they are added up. The sum is then divided by the actual number of starters. This yields an average innings per starting pitcher. Any pitcher who threw at or above the average moves on for further analysis and qualifies to be best starting pitcher, best offensive pitcher, and best defensive pitcher. It is very rare if one pitcher wins all three, but it has occurred. The starting pitchers who do not make the cut are ignored.

For those years where a breakdown of starting innings pitched and relief innings pitched are not available, pitchers are considered who threw at least 15% of their team's total innings.

As with the offensive tabulation, I do not recommend comparing pitchers from different eras. Starters through the deadball era competed under different conditions than starters today. Of course, if you want to go ahead and compare Steve Carlton with Grover Alexander anyway, you have the formula.

Appendix D
Best Starting Pitcher by Season

1871 – George Zettlein

1872 – Dick McBride

1873 – Bobby Mathews

1874 – Bobby Mathews

1875 – Bobby Mathews

1876 – George Bradley

1877 – Tommy Bond

1878 – Tommy Bond

1879 – Will White

1880 – Jim McCormick

1881 – George Derby

1882 – Jim McCormick NL   Tony Mullane AA

1883 – Jim Whitney NL   Tim Keefe AA

1884 – Old Hoss Radbourn NL   Guy Hecker AA

1885 – John Clarkson NL   Bobby Mathews AA

1886 – Lady Baldwin NL   Matt Kilroy AA

1887 – Jim Whitney NL   Toad Ramsey AA

1888 – Tim Keefe NL   Silver King AA

1889 – John Clarkson NL   Mark Baldwin AA

1890 – Kid Gleason NL   Sadie McMahon AA   Harry Staley PL

1891 – Bill Hutchison NL   Sadie McMahon AA

1892 – Bill Hutchison

1893 – Cy Young

4 – Bobby Mathews   2 – Tommy Bond, Jim McCormick, Jim Whitney, Tim Keefe, John Clarkson

Sadie McMahon, Bill Hutchison

Appendix E
Rating Pitchers – Relievers

Relief pitchers are rated somewhat differently than starting pitchers.

Certainly, there are some common elements. The frequency of strikeouts compared to walks and hit batsmen remains critical for relievers, and is probably of greater import given the, often, very limited margin for error. The same would be true for frequency of home runs allowed. But there, I believe, the similarity with starting pitchers ends.

A relief pitcher throws far fewer innings than a frontline starting pitcher. Consequently, it would be ludicrous to apply the same innings pitched standard used for starting pitchers to relief pitchers. Additionally, whereas starting pitchers, at least in the modern era, may pitch every four to five days apart, gifted relief pitchers may pitch in consecutive games for days in succession. Finally, won/lost records for relief pitchers are largely irrelevant. Many wins earned in relief are, in fact, the unintended result of poor relief pitching, i.e., a blown save opportunity. This is not exclusively the case, but it occurs often enough to render wins earned in relief highly dubious.

So here is the formula used to rate relief pitching.

Relief Ks –(W + HBP)/Relief IPs + Relief IPs/Team Relief IPs + Relief Appearances/Team Relief Appearances - Relief HRs Allowed/Relief IPs =

Relief Ks –(W + HBP)/Relief IPs: Nothing new here. Once again, as with starters, the pitcher is penalized by having his walks and hit batsmen deducted from his strikeout total. A negative value can be earned.

Relief IPs/Team Relief IPs: This is the workhorse version of the same stat used for starters, but applied to relief innings only. This ensures that long relievers or set up men are given their due.

Relief Appearances/Team Relief Appearances: The underlying concept here is that only the best relievers pitch frequently.

Relief HRs/Relief IPs: Again, nothing new here. The pitcher is penalized for the frequency of home runs he yields, but only in a relief capacity. As with starters, the best a pitcher can hope to attain in this category is a 0.

So there it is. Let's apply it to two Hall of Fame relievers, Goose Gossage and Bruce Sutter.

Relief Ks −(W + HBP)/RIP + Relief IPs/Team RIPs + Relief Apps/Team Relief Apps - Relief HRs/RIPs =

1978 Gossage NY Yankees

.454 + .325 + .335 - .067 = 1.047

1982 Sutter St. Louis Cards

.234 + .232 + .220 - .078 = 0.608

I deliberately picked seasons in which each pitcher was the ace reliever for the World Series champion and must admit to being surprised at how much better Gossage was than Sutter for his team. I suppose other seasons could provide different results and one can always compare them by plugging in their career numbers. Great fun.

As with starting pitchers, not all relievers are alike. Bruce Sutter, who appeared in 70 games in relief in 1982, ought not be compared with teammate Eric Rasmussen, who relieved in 5. For each season I collect the total appearances made by all relievers in each league and divide by the number of relievers. This yields an average of appearances made in each league. Any reliever with the average number of appearances or above is considered to be in the running for best reliever in his league. The rest are ignored for their relief output. Relief pitchers are not specifically rated for offense or defense unless they otherwise qualified as a starting pitcher in that season. This is due to the very limited nature of their appearances. It is possible for a pitcher to accomplish being both best starter and best reliever in the same season. It has happened.

You may have noticed that nifty relief stats like saves or 'inherited runners scored' are ignored in my formulation. The reason for that is that those stats are frequently dependent on the support of fielders. All the stats I use in the relief pitcher evaluation are pitcher specific, excepting for the occurrence of inside-the-park home runs, which I cannot trace back to the pitcher.

Please note that breakdowns of innings pitched in a starting or relief capacity are not generally available prior to 1901. For that period, while we know how many games a pitcher threw in relief, we do not know how many relief innings he threw or what he did in them. As a consequence, a best reliever for most of the years prior to 1901 cannot be chosen. Happily, relief pitching was not nearly as pervasive for that period as in the present day.

So that's it for relief pitching. As with offense and starting pitchers, I do not think it is appropriate to compare relief pitchers from the present era with relievers from even as recently as the 1970's. A lot has changed in the way relievers are used and the conditions under which they pitch spanning different eras. Of course, that being said, there is nothing to stop you from comparing Firpo Marberry with Sparky Lyle just for fun. You have the formula.

Appendix F
Assessing Defense

Defense is assessed the same way for all full-time fielders, unless they are multi-position players. Defense is not assessed for multi-position players. More on that later.

If you are a baseball fan you probably have some familiarity with various fielding stats, like putouts, assists, and errors. In each of these categories someone has the most, and someone else has the least, for better or worse. By that I mean, someone has the most assists, which is good. Someone else has the least assists, which is bad. Someone has the most errors, which is bad. Someone else has the least errors, which is good.

I examine six key categories for every fielder, determine whether he was the best or the worst in each category, and award a point or deduct a point depending on the outcome. If he was neither the best nor the worst, he receives a neutral zero. Once all the categories have been graded, they are added up and a value for the season is assigned.

Six categories are examined for each such fielder. Seven for catchers. The six categories are; putouts, assists, errors, total chances per inning, fielding percentage (the percentage of successful, errorless chances divided by all chances), and double plays. Catchers are also evaluated on their caught stealing percentage, where it is available. When calculating errors for catchers, passed balls are taken into account. When calculating errors for pitchers, wild pitches are taken into account. This is because passed balls and wild pitches are not scored as errors, but they are, nonetheless.

So the best a player can score defensively in a season is 6. The worst he can score is a -6. The best a catcher can score is a 7. The worst a catcher can score is, you guessed it, a -7. A certain balance is built into this method of assessing defense. Often enough the fielders with the most putouts and assists are the ones with the most errors and lower fielding percentages. This is not always the case, but the guy with the most is not necessarily going to score the best.

I use total chances per inning instead of total chances per game because total chances per inning is more accurate. Players frequently do not play a whole game when they appear in one.

It's always more fun to illustrate. As of this writing, there is some chatter about Derek Jeter's defensive ability concerning his election to the Hall of Fame. Many commentators believe he was not very good defensively. I always thought he was an excellent defender, watching him play consistently for his entire career. So let's take a random season for Derek, and compare him with his peers using the method I have outlined above. Let's examine 1997, a random year.

First we have to determine who the full-time AL shortstops were that year. In order to qualify as a full-time shortstop the player had to play shortstop for at least 75% of his team's innings played. Jeter played 1,417 innings at shortstop that season. The Yankees played 1,467.67 innings in total. That works out to 96% shortstop innings for Jeter. The remaining full-time shortstops in the AL were Mike Bordick, Deivi Cruz, Nomar Garciaparra, Alex Gonzalez, Omar Vizquel, Ozzie Guillen, Jose Valentin, Pat Meares, Jay Bell, Alex Rodriguez, and Gary DiSarcina. That's quite a mob. Because there are more than 5, the top two at each category will receive a point. The bottom two in each category will have a point deducted. This also might be the most number of z's at any position I have charted.

So here are the shortstops:

Jeter, Bordick, Cruz, Garciaparra, Gonzalez, Vizquel, Guillen, Valentin, Meares, Bell, Rodriguez, DiSarcina

Here is the grid. Remember, the top two in each category get a point, the bottom two have a point deducted. The rest get zeros. Stats used are from Baseball Reference.com and Retrosheet.org. In the 'Errors' category the players with the least errors are on top on the grid.

Putouts	Assists	Errors	Total Chances/Inning	Percentage	DPs
Garciaparra	Jeter	Gonzalez	Meares	Gonzalez	Garciaparra
Vizquel	Garciaparra	Bell/Vizquel	Garciaparra	Vizquel	Bell
Cruz	Gonzalez	Rodriguez	Guillen	Rodriguez	Gonzalez
Guillen	Guillen	Garciaparra	Bordick	Valentin	Guillen

Now we total up the scores. Full credit for a tie.

Garciaparra 3   Jeter 1   Gonzalez 0   Meares 1   Vizquel 3   Bell 2   Cruz -1   Rodriguez -2

Guillen -4   Bordick -1   Valentin -1   DiSarcina 0

So there you have it. Nomar and Vizquel were the best AL shortstops in 1997. Guillen, at age 33 and near the end of his career was the worst. Jeter was in the middle of the pack. Notice that Nomar was in the top 2 in both putouts and assists, but also among the worst 2 in errors. DPs are always kind of a wild card.

As I mentioned earlier, with more than 5 players at a position, the top 2 and bottom 2 get or lose points, otherwise it's just the single best and the single worst. Also, no ties are allowed in a category with less than 8 players. In that circumstance there is a nil.

At the outset I made reference to multi-position players. Because multi-position players do not play at least 75% of the time at any single position, they do not qualify to have their defense assessed. The reason for this is that the results would be skewed. The multi-position player would lose in most categories, excepting, most likely, errors. He doesn't deserve to lose or to receive a negative rating merely because he didn't play full-time at the position, so he ends up only being counted for offense in the category of multi-position player. There is a best multi-position player every season on offense.

Catchers encounter a great deal of difficulty in playing 75% of their team's innings at catcher. Consequently, the bar for catchers is lowered to 66% of their team's innings played.

So there you have it. If you want to take the time, you can run an assessment for any player for each year of his career in which he played full-time, add up all the seasonal numbers, and then divide by the number of seasons. This would give you a lifetime defensive rating for the player. I wonder if Jeter has a better lifetime rating than Honus Wagner?

Appendix G
Source Materials

This grand opus is entitled 'Big League Baseball, A History', with an emphasis on the A. The book is not and does not claim to be the definitive history of major league baseball. As stated in the Preface to volume I, the focus of these volumes is limited to important developments in the evolution of the game from the commencement of league play in 1871, outstanding players at their position every year, exciting pennant races, post – season play and its development, and some statistical analysis. Although a bibliography is attached a few words are appropriate regarding source materials.

Statistics

The first statistical compilations I was exposed to were on the backs of baseball cards. I never questioned the accuracy of the data and spent many hours as a child poring over every line. In about 1980 I became aware of the existence of The Baseball Encyclopedia. It was at this time that the genesis of the work you are presently reading occurred. The Baseball Encyclopedia became my Rosetta Stone and I have literally spent decades seeking to untangle and re-interpret its mysteries.

Well, things change. The internet has rendered the encyclopedia nearly obsolete and I have learned that not everything on the printed page is to be believed. Internet sources such as Retrosheet and Baseball Reference now form the basis for my statistical research. Retrosheet, in particular, has been a critical source as its researchers study box scores and play by play accounts, both of which are statistical bedrock, in arriving at player production totals.

I have striven during the course of my statistical research to be as accurate as the source materials allow me to be. Where I have encountered inconsistencies between sources in the statistical record I have used what I consider to be the most accurate. In this respect the season splits available at Retrosheet, which frequently disagree with the official stats issued by Major League Baseball, have proven most valuable. I have also referenced detailed updates provided from time to time through research conducted by members of SABR, the Society for American Baseball Research.

The statistics which form the basis of my player formulas are the most accurate available. I have not done any guesstimating or speculating when it comes to the statistical record. I am confident that my production formulas are based on the most accurate statistical data available.

Individual Games

The best sources for individual games are box scores accompanied by game accounts. Sometimes they are available at Retrosheet. Sometimes newspaper accounts must be consulted, when they can be found. The Library of Congress website has many newspapers available on its search engine. I have consulted 19th century German language newspapers from the Baltimore area for their box scores when questions of accuracy have arisen. Happily, McGraw is spelled the same in German as in English. Various digital collections of vintage publications are available on the internet. Issues of the New York Clipper can be found on the website of the Illinois Digital Newspaper Collection. The Sporting Life archive is maintained by the LA84 Digital Library. Newspapers.com is another source for game accounts and box scores, for a monthly fee (free for SABR members). 'Great game' accounts have also recently been collected in book format by SABR. The SABR Games Project also provides detailed accounts of individual games. When nothing more than box scores are available I work with what I have. In such cases I do not speculate that a single was a screaming liner or a blooper.

Pennant Races

Retrosheet maintains a game log which provides standings on a day by day basis. In this way, I can track winning/losing streaks and pennant races. Book length treatments also exist for historic pennant races and seasons.

Post Season

Multiple sources are available for the post season including Retrosheet, Baseball Reference, encyclopedias, and book length treatments. Starting in the late 1970s I can also provide personal, eyewitness accounts of certain post-season events.

History

I was born in 1956 and attended my first ballgame with the Cub Scouts in 1965, a Mets game against Cincinnati at Shea Stadium. I had baseball cards in 1964 or 1965 and probably started reading the newspaper in 1966. The first World Series I have any memory of was in 1967, Boston against St. Louis. The point is, I could not have been an eyewitness to anything that occurred in the baseball world before the mid 1960's.

Consequently, I have resorted to various publications to provide information about the events described in the text of this book. Commonly, I have reviewed multiple sources for each season or era and synthesized what I felt important for inclusion in each chapter. The specific publications I have used are attributed in the bibliography. In this respect I have, without question, ridden on the shoulders of those who have gone before me. I am indebted to my predecessors and thank them for the hours they provided me in baseball's time machine.

Certain books have become available in recent years which document changes in the game. These publications provide information regarding big league baseball annual meetings and the evolution in equipment and day to day practices. Copies of National League rule books, which contain minutes of League meetings dating back to the 19th century, can be found at in the digital collection of the University of Maryland Library. Such publications are of immense value. Once again, they are attributed in the bibliography.

I expect that as this book progresses new source materials will become available. While it is too late to go backwards I will always endeavor to provide the most recent baseball scholarship in support of my research.

I encourage anyone with an interest in specific subjects which I have glossed over in the text to follow up with more topic intensive source materials which are referenced in the bibliography.

Thanks for reading. I hope you have enjoyed the experience

Appendix H
The Pictures

This is not the first book written about the chronological history of baseball. Previous such books have, more often than not, utilized grainy, over or under exposed black and white photographs to depict images of the players. While I applaud the efforts of my predecessors and their use of 19th century state of the art photography, I wanted to do better.

As I have previously mentioned, I began collecting baseball cards around 1964 or 1965 when I was about 8 years old. For me baseball cards were the windows to the likenesses and personalities of the players. Today, half a century after I started collecting baseball cards, I continue to find them the most intimate, up close and personal opportunity for the average fan to experience a player. Furthermore, yearly issues of baseball cards constitute a recurring, high quality pictorial database for the players. As a consequence, I resolved to use only baseball cards as the illustrations to my chapters.

Baseball cards existed in the 19th century in various forms, but most popularly as tobacco cards, that is to say, individual baseball cards, running the gamut of quality, issued with packs of cigarettes. In recent years Jesse Loving of Ars Longa Cards has updated 19th century cards with backgrounds and color to create the kind of intimate player depiction that was not possible at the time of the issuance of the original card. I tracked down Mr. Loving, and was thrilled to obtain permission to use his cards to illustrate the early volumes.

Now don't get me wrong. I have nothing against black and white photography. In fact, in future volumes I anticipate extensive use of high quality black and white baseball cards from the Conlon Collection. But the keyword here is *quality*. The cards issued by Ars Longa represent the highest *quality* images of their subjects available at the present time. In my opinion these images bring the players depicted thereon to life in a way that simply was not possible with 19th century photography. As one of the goals of this book is to recall the greatness and popularity of bygone players, you, and they, deserve nothing less than the best effort at trying to illustrate their personalities and restore them in the imagination as living persons. I believe the use of these baseball cards as illustrations serves to accomplish that goal.

As examples, consider that the biography of Cherokee Fisher is written into his face on the card used for 1874. Witness the cocky self-assuredness of Ross Barnes on both of his cards used for 1875 and 1876. Harry Wright is rectitude personified in the card used for 1871, while William Hulbert brings to mind something completely different on his card for 1880.

When you regard the baseball cards in these volumes, please pause for a few moments while you examine the features of the players. Look into their eyes, observe their grinning or dour countenances, see if you can discover the essence of the man. See if you can perceive a glimmer of his soul.

For more information on Jesse Loving and Ars Longa cards go to arslongaartcards.com.

Appendix I
Artwork Credits

Front Cover - Design by Jesse Loving. Main image adapted from St. George Grounds, The Hatch Litho Co., 1886, Library of Congress, Prints & Photographs Division.

Features the cards:

    Reilly and Nicol (Long and Short): Ars Longa Art Cards 'Diamond Duos'

    Will White: Ars Longa Art Cards 'Beginnings: 1880s' *

    Matt Kilroy: Ars Longa Art Cards 'Beginnings: 1880s'

    Williamson and Hahm: Ars Longa Art Cards 'Diamond Duos'

Introduction - James Creighton: Ars Longa Art Cards 'Excelsior of Brooklyn:1860 Cabinet' *

1871 - Dick McBride: Ars Longa Art Cards 'Athletic of Philadelphia: 1874'

Harry Wright: Ars Longa Art Cards 'Boston Red Stockings Cabinet, Type II' *

1872 - Charlie Gould: Ars Longa Art Cards 'Mort's Reserve' #10

Ross Barnes: Ars Longa Art Cards 'Spearheads' *

Albert Spalding: Ars Longa Art Cards 'Spearheads'

George Wright: Ars Longa Art Cards 'Spearheads'

Harry Schafer: Ars Longa Art Cards 'Mort's Reserve' #24

1873 - Bob Addy: Ars Longa Art Cards 'Pioneer Portraits I' #20

Albert Spalding: Ars Longa Art Cards 'Boston Red Stockings Cabinet, Type II' *

1874 - Cherokee Fisher: Ars Longa Art Cards 'Mort's Reserve' #5

1875 - Albert Spalding: Ars Longa Art Cards 'Mort's Reserve' #23 *

Deacon White: Ars Longa Art Cards 'Mort's Reserve' #69 *

Cal McVey: Ars Longa Art Cards 'Mort's Reserve' #4

Ross Barnes: Ars Longa Art Cards 'Boston Red Stockings Cabinet, Type I' *

Harry Schafer: Ars Longa Art Cards 'Mort's Reserve' #33 *

George Wright: Ars Longa Art Cards 'Mort's Reserve' #26

Andy Leonard: Ars Longa Art Cards 'Mort's Reserve' #62

Jim O'Rourke: Ars Longa Art Cards 'Mort's Reserve' #44

Jack Manning: Ars Longa Art Cards 'Mort's Reserve' #58

1876 - Ross Barnes: Ars Longa Art Cards 'Pioneer Portraits II'

1877 - Deacon White: Ars Longa Art Cards 'Pioneer Portraits II'

Tommy Bond: Ars Longa Art Cards 'Beginnings: 1880s'

1878 - Harry Wright: Ars Longa Art Cards 'Pioneer Portraits I'

Cap Anson: Ars Longa Art Cards 'Pioneer Portraits I' *

Tommy Bond: Ars Longa Art Cards 'Pioneer Portraits I'

1879 - Paul Hines: Ars Longa Art Cards 'Beginnings: 1880s'

Charley Jones: Ars Longa Art Cards 'Pioneer Portraits II'

George Wright: Ars Longa Art Cards 'Boston Red Stockings Cabinet, Type II' *

Tom York: Ars Longa Art Cards 'Pioneer Portraits I'

1880 - Abner Dalrymple: Ars Longa Art Cards 'Beginnings: 1880s'

Jim McCormick: Ars Longa Art Cards 'Beginnings: 1880s'

William Hulbert: Ars Longa Art Cards 'Pioneer Portraits II'

1881 - Abner Dalrymple: Ars Longa Art Cards 'Pioneer Portraits II'

George Gore: Ars Longa Art Cards 'Pioneer Portraits II'

Mike Kelly: Ars Longa Art Cards 'Pioneer Portraits II'

Larry Corcoran: Ars Longa Art Cards 'Beginnings: 1880s'

Cap Anson: Ars Longa Art Cards 'Beginnings: 1880s'

1882 - Hick Carpenter: Ars Longa Art Cards 'Beginnings: 1880s'

Bid McPhee: Ars Longa Art Cards 'Beginnings: 1880s'

Jimmy Macullar: Ars Longa Art Cards 'Beginnings: 1880s'

1883 - John Reilly: Ars Longa Art Cards 'Beginnings: 1880s'

'Grasshopper' Whitney: Ars Longa Art Cards 'Pioneer Portraits II'

1884 - Guy Hecker: Ars Longa Art Cards 'Beginnings: 1880s'

Dave Orr: Ars Longa Art Cards 'Beginnings: 1880s > Spotted Ties'

Charles Radbourn: Ars Longa Art Cards 'Loving Cabinet' *

1885 - John Clarkson: Ars Longa Art Cards 'Pioneer Portraits II'

Bobby Mathews: Ars Longa Art Cards 'Beginnings: 1880s'

Cap Anson: Ars Longa Art Cards 'Pioneer Portraits II'

1886 - Curt Welch: Ars Longa Art Cards 'Beginnings: 1880s'

Arlie Latham: Ars Longa Art Cards 'Beginnings: 1880s'

Charles Comiskey: Ars Longa Art Cards 'Beginnings: 1880s'

Bob Caruthers: Ars Longa Art Cards 'Beginnings: 1880s'

1887 - Sam Thompson: Ars Longa Art Cards 'Pioneer Portraits II'

Dan Brouthers: Ars Longa Art Cards 'Pioneer Portraits II'

King Solomon White: Ars Longa Art Cards 'NLBGM Dedication' *

1888 - Silver King: Ars Longa Art Cards 'Beginnings: 1880s'

Tim Keefe: Ars Longa Art Cards 'Beginnings: 1880s'

Chris von der Ahe: Ars Longa Art Cards 'Beginnings: 1880's'

1889 - John Ward: Ars Longa Art Cards 'Beginnings: 1880s'

Roger Connor: Ars Longa Art Cards 'Loving Pauper'

Hank O'Day: Ars Longa Art Cards 'Pioneer Portraits II'

1890 - Hardy Richardson: Ars Longa Art Cards 'Pioneer Portraits II'

Oyster Burns: Ars Longa Art Cards 'Beginnings: 1880s'

Chicken Wolf: Ars Longa Art Cards 'Beginnings: 1880s'

1891 - Harry Stovey: Ars Longa Art Cards 'Beginnings: 1880s'

Tom Brown: Ars Longa Art Cards 'Pioneer Portraits II'

1892 - Bill Hutchison: Ars Longa Art Cards 'Beginnings: 1880s'

Hugh Duffy: Ars Longa Art Cards 'Beginnings: 1880s' *

Dan Brouthers: Ars Longa Art Cards 'Loving Pauper' *

1893 - Ed Delahanty: Ars Longa Art Cards 'Pioneer Portraits II'

Cy Young: Ars Longa Art Cards 'Cleveland BBC by Jousts' *

Back Cover - Design by Jesse Loving. Main image adapted from The Polo Grounds, New York Litho Co., 1887, Library of Congress, Prints & Photographs Division.

Features the cards:

> Farrell tags Hines: Ars Longa Art Cards 'Diamond Duos'
>
> Hoover tags Andrews: Ars Longa Art Cards 'Diamond Duos'

* Denotes artwork loaned to or created specifically for this publication that may or may not otherwise be available to view or collect through Ars Longa Art Cards

BIBLIOGRAPHY TO VOLUME 1

On-line Sources

Retrosheet.org – The information used here was obtained free of charge from and is copyrighted by Retrosheet. Interested parties may contact Retrosheet at www.retrosheet.org.

Sports Reference LLC – Baseball-Reference.com – Major League Statistics and Information. https://baseball-reference.com/.

SABR.org – https://sabr.org/the-research-collection/

New York Clipper – https://digital.library.illinois.edu/collections/4f495de0-b7e2-0133-1d02-0050569601ca-4

Newspapers.com – https://www.newspapers.com

The Library of Congress – https://chroniclingamerica.loc.gov

University of Maryland Library – https://www.lib.umd.edu/collections/university-archives/digital/baseball-rules

Books

Achorn, Edward, Fifty-nine in '84, New York: Smithsonian Books, 2010.

Alexander, Charles, Turbulent Seasons in Baseball 1890-1891, Dallas: Southern Methodist University Press, 2011.

Bevis, Charlie, Tim Keefe: A Biography of the Hall of Fame Pitcher and Player-Rights Advocate, Jefferson, NC: McFarland & Company, Inc., 2015.

Hodges, Jeremy K. and Nowlin, Bill, eds., Baseball's 19th Century Winter Meetings 1857-1900, Phoenix: Society for American Baseball Research, Inc., 2018.

Bucek, Jeanine, ed., The Baseball Encyclopedia, New York: MacMillan, 1996.

Dewan, John and James, Bill and Munro, Neil and Zminda, Don, eds., STATS All-Time Baseball Sourcebook, Skokie, IL: STATS, Inc., 1998.

Di Salvatore, Bryan, A Clever Base-Ballist: The Life and times of John Montgomery Ward, New York: Pantheon Books, 1999.

Felber, Bill, ed., Inventing Baseball: The 100 Greatest Games of the Nineteenth Century, Phoenix: Society for American Baseball Research, Inc., 2013.

Gershman, Michael and Palmer, Pete and Pietrusza, David and Thorn, John, eds., Total Baseball, New York: Total Sports, 1999.

Goldstein, Warren, A History of Early Baseball: Playing for Keeps: 1857-1876, New York: Barnes & Noble Books, 2000.

Graf, John, ed., From Rube to Robinson: SABR's Best Articles on Black Baseball, Phoenix: Society for American Baseball Research, Inc., 2020.

Guschov, Stephen D., The Red Stockings of Cincinnati, Jefferson, NC: McFarland & Company, Inc., 1998.

Hershberger, Richard, Strike Four: The Evolution of Baseball, Lanham, MD: Rowman & Littlefield, 2019.

James, Bill, The New Bill James Historical Baseball Abstract, New York: The Free Press, 2001

James, Bill, The Bill James Guide to Baseball Managers from 1870 to Today, New York: Scribner, 1997.

LeMoine, Bob and Nowlin, Bill, eds., Boston's First Nine: The 1871-75 Boston Red Stockings, Phoenix: Society for American Baseball Research, Inc., 2016.

Lowry, Phillip J., Green Cathedrals, Cooperstown: Society for American Baseball Research, 1986.

Melville, Tom, Early Baseball and the Rise of the National League, Jefferson, NC: McFarland & Company, Inc., 2001.

Nemec, David, The Beer and Whisky League, New York: Lyons & Burford, 1994.

Nemec, David, The Great Encyclopedia of 19th Century Major League Baseball, New York: Donald I. Fine Books, 1997.

Orem, Preston D., Baseball (1882-1891) From the Newspaper Accounts, Altadena, CA: Preston D. Orem, 1967, distributed by SABR 19th Century Research Committee, 2021.

Ryczek, William J., Blackguards and Red Stockings, Wallingford, CT: Colebrook Press, 1999.

Seymour, Harold and Seymour, Dorothy Z., Baseball: The Early Years, New York: Oxford University Press, 1989.

Tiemann, Robert L. and Rucker, Mark, eds., <u>Nineteenth Century Stars</u>, Kansas City: The Society for American Baseball research, Inc., 1989.

Voight, David Quentin, <u>American Baseball From the Gentleman's Sport to the Commissioner System :Volume I</u>, University Park, PA: The Pennsylvania State University Press, 1983.

Wright, Marshall D., <u>Nineteenth Century Baseball</u>, Jefferson, NC: McFarland, 1996.

White, Sol, <u>Sol White's History of Colored Baseball</u>, Las Vegas: Bison Books, 2021.

Articles

Bailey, Bob, ed., Pajot, Dennis, <u>Baseball's First World Series Goat</u>, Nineteenth Century Notes, Spring 2009,pp8-12, Society for American Baseball Research, 2009.

Hershberger, Richard, <u>The First Baseball War: The American Association and the National League</u>, Baseball Research Journal, Fall 2020, pp115-125, Phoenix: The Society for American Baseball Research, Inc., 2020.

Ivor-Campbell, Frederick, ed., Payne, Martin, <u>Never Behind the Times</u>, Nineteenth Century Notes, 99:2 Spring 1999, Society for American Baseball Research, 1999.

Wendt, Paul, ed., <u>That Was Baseball Then</u>, Nineteenth Century Notes, 2005:1, pp1-3, Society for American Baseball Research, 2005.